The Yoga Within You

Living Beyond the Mat

Jenny Guzon-Bae

For more information, email yogawithinyouretreats@gmail.com

Cover Design by Sumara Fireside of Design Fireside

Interior Design by Sherri Marteney

Edited by Chiara Torelli

ISBN: 9798872356202

Dedications

To my parents, Jesus & Corazon Guzon, your commitment to instilling in me the values of hard work, resilience, and determination has been the cornerstone of my journey. You both taught me that success is not merely a destination but a result of relentless effort and dedication.

I am eternally grateful for the sacrifices you have made, the countless hours you have dedicated to my growth, and the unconditional love you have showered upon me.

This book is a testament to the invaluable life lessons you have imparted upon me, the inspiration you have instilled, and the support you have provided throughout my journey.

Thank you with all my love.

To my husband, Don, and my son, Casey, you are both my pillars of strength, my constant sources of support, and the driving forces behind my journey. You have been my cheerleaders and the source of endless love and inspiration that has propelled me forward.

Don, your steadfast support and encouragement have been the foundation upon which I have built my dreams. You have believed in me from the beginning, even when I doubted myself. Your faith in my abilities has given me the confidence to pursue my passions fearlessly. You have always been there to lift me up when I stumbled, to celebrate my victories, and to remind me of my worth even in moments of self-doubt. Your love and belief in me have been the wind beneath my wings, and I am forever grateful for your presence in my life.

Casey, you are my greatest source of inspiration. Watching you grow has been a constant reminder of the beauty and potential that lies within each of us. Your kind heart and unwavering loyalty to those you hold dear are a constant reminder that there is goodness in the world. You have given me the courage to dream bigger, to push beyond my limits, and to embrace the unknown with open arms. As I strive to be an inspiration to you, know that you have already inspired me in countless ways.

Both of you have given me the space to grow, to explore my passions, and to chase my dreams. You have never held me back, but instead, you have always encouraged me to reach for the stars. Your support has allowed me to spread my wings and soar to new heights. Your love has been the anchor that keeps me grounded, even in the face of life's challenges.

This book reflects the lessons I have learned from both of you and the inspiration you have provided. Thank you both for being my rock, motivation, and greatest source of love and encouragement. I dedicate this book to you with all my heart, hoping it serves as a reminder of the profound impact you have had on my life.

Contents

Contents

Contents

Contents

Contents

Contents

Contents

Introduction

IN THE HUSTLE AND bustle of our modern lives, we often yearn for a deeper connection, a sense of purpose, and a path leading us toward a more meaningful existence. Within the profound teachings of yoga philosophy, we discover the wisdom and tools to navigate this journey.

For over two decades, I have immersed myself in the practice of yoga, exploring its physical, mental, and spiritual dimensions. Before that, however, I lived a different life - a wife, mother to a pre-teen, and real estate agent trying to do everything perfectly. Superficially, life was good, but I wanted more. I was somehow meant to do more.

In 2006, I was selected to compete on the CBS reality competition show, Survivor: Cook Islands. Embarking on the adventure of a lifetime is a challenging feat. The physical and mental challenges, the intense competition, and the constant uncertainty can push even the strongest individuals to their limits. During my time on the show, I discovered that leaning onto my yoga practice became my anchor, providing me with the strength, resilience, and inner peace necessary to endure the challenges of the game.

Yoga taught me the importance of connecting my mind and body, allowing me to stay grounded and focused amidst the chaos. Through breathwork and mindful movement, I was able to calm my racing thoughts, find clarity, and make better decisions. Whether it was during physically demanding challenges or moments of strategic planning, yoga helped me stay present and centered.

My experience on Survivor was undoubtedly one of the most challenging and transformative periods of my life. Through the practice of yoga, I discovered an inner strength, resilience, and peace that helped me navigate the physical, mental, and emotional hurdles that came my way. Yoga became my guiding light, allowing me to endure the challenges, stay grounded, and embrace the journey with grace and gratitude. Whether on a reality show or in everyday life, yoga has the power to empower us to face any challenge that comes our way.

I lasted 25 of 39 days on Survivor. I did not win $1 million, but I gained much more from that experience. Little did I know that this adventure would also ignite a profound realization within me—that my career path was not aligned with my true purpose. Through self-reflection and soul-searching, I discovered that teaching yoga was my *dharma*, often referred to as one's true calling or purpose and the path I was meant to follow.

With newfound clarity, I quit real estate and embarked on a journey to become a certified yoga teacher. I immersed myself in intensive training, deepening my knowledge of yoga philosophy, asanas, and teaching methodologies. The more I learned, the more I realized that teaching yoga was not just a profession but a way of life, a means to inspire and empower others.

As a dedicated practitioner and yoga instructor since 2008, I have witnessed firsthand the transformative power of yoga philosophy in my own life and the lives of countless others. Through these experiences, I have come to understand the profound impact that yoga can have on our everyday lives.

In this book, I invite you to join me on a journey of self-discovery and self-transformation as we explore the nuggets of knowledge derived from yoga philosophy and learn how to apply them to our everyday lives. Drawing from my experiences as a practitioner and guide, I will share insights that can help you navigate the challenges and complexities of modern life.

Yoga philosophy offers us a holistic approach to living, encompassing not only physical postures but also ethical principles, meditation practices, and a deep understanding of our true nature. It invites us to explore the depths of our being, cultivate self-awareness, and align our actions with our highest values.

My journey with yoga has been profound, shaping my life and guiding me toward better decisions and a deeper connection with the Divine. Through the practice of yoga, I have learned to cultivate compassion, patience, and resilience. I have discovered the power of surrender and the beauty of living in the present moment. Yoga has become not just a physical practice but a way of life, a path that leads me toward a greater sense of purpose and fulfillment.

Throughout this book, we will delve into key concepts such as the Yamas and Niyamas, the ethical principles that guide our interactions with ourselves and others. We will explore the power of breathwork, learn to quiet the mind, and connect with our inner wisdom. We will also delve into some of the teachings of the Bhagavad Gita and the Yoga Sutras, uncovering timeless wisdom that can guide us towards a life lived in harmony with the Divine.

As we embark on this exploration of yoga philosophy, let us remember that the true essence of these teachings lies not in intellectual understanding alone but in their practical application to our everyday lives. Through consistent practice and sincere dedication, we can unlock the transformative power of yoga and experience its profound impact on our well-being.

May this book serve as a companion on your journey, offering insights, inspiration, and practical guidance as you apply the teachings of yoga philosophy to your daily life. Embrace the wisdom of the ancients and embark on a path of self-discovery, self-transformation, and, ultimately, a life lived with greater purpose and fulfillment so that you may find The Yoga Within You.

Introduction to "Pranayama Pause"

I STRONGLY BELIEVE IN the power of the breath as a transformative tool in yoga, meditation, and everyday life. The breath serves as a bridge between the body and mind, allowing us to tap into our inner wisdom, find stillness amidst chaos, and cultivate a sense of presence and awareness. Through the practice of pranayama, we can harness the inherent power of the breath to prepare ourselves for meditation, deepen our yoga practice, and navigate the challenges and joys of life with grace and resilience.

Throughout the pages of this book, you will find sporadic pauses, inviting you to engage in various pranayama techniques. These pauses are strategically placed to encourage you to take a break from reading, connect with your breath, and experience the profound effects of conscious breathing firsthand. By integrating these pauses into your reading experience, you will gain knowledge about pranayama and the opportunity to embody its teachings in real time.

What is Pranayama?

Pranayama is a Sanskrit term meaning "extension of life force" or "control of breath." It is a fundamental aspect of yoga, focusing on conscious regulation and manipulation of the breath to influence the flow of prana (life force energy) within the body. Pranayama techniques involve specific breathing patterns, rhythms, and breath retention to balance and harmonize the body, mind, and spirit.

Benefits of Pranayama:

Pranayama offers a multitude of benefits that extend beyond the physical realm. By incorporating pranayama into your yoga practice, meditation, or daily life, you can experience:

1. Enhanced breath awareness: Pranayama cultivates a deep connection with the breath, allowing you to become more attuned to its subtle nuances and rhythms.

2. Stress reduction: The deliberate and conscious breathing techniques of pranayama activate the parasympathetic nervous system, promoting relaxation, reducing stress, and calming the mind.

3. Improved mental clarity and focus: Pranayama practices oxygenate the brain, increasing mental clarity, focus, and concentration.

4. Increased energy and vitality: By optimizing the breath, pranayama techniques help to increase energy levels, invigorate the body, and awaken dormant energy within.

5. Emotional balance: Pranayama can help regulate emotions, reduce anxiety, and promote emotional well-being.

Contraindications:

While pranayama offers numerous benefits, it is essential to approach the practice with caution and respect for your body's limitations. Some pranayama techniques may not be suitable for individuals with certain medical conditions, such as high blood pressure, heart problems, respiratory disorders, or if you are pregnant. It is advisable to consult with a qualified healthcare professional before engaging in pranayama, especially if you have any pre-existing health concerns.

Part One

Illusion

ACCORDING TO VEDIC TEXTS, *MAYA is an illusion where things appear to be present but are not what they seem.*

Why do we do what we do? Why do we struggle to achieve things that don't bring out the best in us? Why do we struggle to fit into societies and situations that don't bring us joy? Whose criteria do we measure our success by?

Today we exist in a world of appearances and influences, where the treatment and respect we receive depends on our ability to conform effectively, and we constantly compare ourselves with our perception of others.

It feels so important to belong and succeed that we forget what belonging and success really mean to us.

Often, we find that our sense of fulfillment has nothing to do with how we are being told to live our lives and measure our success. The traditional path to success is simply an illusion we buy into so that we can fit in effectively and easily. It stops us having to ask the difficult questions: What do I want? What brings me fulfillment?

We don't need the latest tech, the expensive car, and the fancy clothes. We don't need the flashy apartment or the massive house. We don't need the 24/7 high-powered job.

Look beyond the illusion to find your Truth and your Joy. Look at your relationship with the people and objects in your life. Look at your relationship with your mind and your body. Look at how you are connected to the Universe in so many beautiful ways. Open yourself to the understanding that there is more to you, more to the world, than meets the eye.

Step away from the rat race, from the illusion of success and happiness. You'll find the balance that enables you to flourish and enables you to lead a fulfilling life of meaning and impact.

Perspective

SOME DAYS, YOU JUST have to be able to see the world from a different point of view. Maybe even turn it upside down.

There are so many things that are simply not within our control: other people's behavior, events that happen to us--even the weather! But there is one thing that is always within our power: Perspective.

If we come at life from the right angle, most everything can be seen in a positive, or at least constructive, light. What have we gained today? How have we been strengthened today? What have we learned?

Changing the way we look at things is the key ingredient in our spiritual and emotional growth, in the magical and wonderful journey that brings us closer to ourselves.

Choosing to see the world from the perspective of Love — Love for ourselves, Love for others, Divine Love — empowers us to grow from every little thing that happens to us, no matter how insignificant or negative it may seem on the surface.

If things aren't going your way...

If it feels like the world is ganging up on you right now...

If the blessings seem fewer than the hardships...

Act on your power to choose how you understand the world.

Choose to see things differently.

Choose Love.

Empower yourself by focusing on what you can control: your perspective.

Growing

GROWTH IS HARD. IT can be uncomfortable. It can be scary.

Whether we can see where we need to be or have no idea what our next steps are, some days it's so much easier to sit snugly in our comfort zone.

Our comfort zone may not be perfect — it doesn't fulfill us, and we know it's not healthy in the long run — but we know it so well. We know where we stand, we know how to act, we know how things go.

Somedays, the only thing scarier than the thought of staying in our comfort zone forever is the thought of the unknown.

And yet, reaching for the unknown is the only way to grow. Stepping bravely into the discomfort and fear that come with Change and Transformation is the first step on your path to a life of Meaning and Impact.

Bravery is not the absence of fear but taking action despite it.

Don't dread or avoid fear and discomfort. Breathe into it and see it for what it is: a sign that you are changing, growing, transforming. Moving forward and evolving. Diving deeper into yourself and expanding the way you exist in this world. It's a sign that you are pushing the boundaries that have been holding you back.

The world is ready for you to break out of the cocoon of your comfort zone, transformed by your own courage and vision. The world is ready for you to step into your life with purpose and intent. You are ready too.

Emotional Maturity

EMOTIONS OFTEN GET A bad reputation. We are taught to suppress or ignore them, fearing that they may cloud our judgment or lead us astray. However, embracing emotional maturity means recognizing that our feelings hold valuable wisdom and insights. Just as our thoughts provide information, our emotions too carry messages that can guide us towards growth and understanding.

Yoga teaches us that emotions are not to be dismissed or suppressed but rather seen as valuable sources of information. Just as our thoughts reflect our mental state, our emotions reflect our inner landscape. They provide us with clues about our needs, desires, and boundaries. By acknowledging and listening to our emotions, we can gain a deeper understanding of ourselves and make more conscious choices.

Amid strong emotions, our instinctive reaction is often to act impulsively or suppress them altogether. However, our yoga practice encourages us to pause and slow down when emotions arise. By taking a moment to breathe and observe, we create space for self-reflection and allow ourselves to respond rather than react. This practice of slowing down helps us cultivate emotional intelligence and make choices aligned with our values.

Yoga teaches us to cultivate awareness in all aspects of our lives, including our emotions. By practicing mindfulness and self-observation, we can develop a deeper understanding of our emotional patterns and triggers. This awareness allows us to respond to our emotions with compassion and curiosity, rather than being overwhelmed by their energy. Through regular practice, we can become more attuned to the wisdom within our feelings.

The concept of *Santosha,* or contentment, reminds us to find peace within ourselves, regardless of external circumstances. By embracing this philosophy, we can approach our emotions with acceptance and non-judgment, allowing us to learn from them rather than being consumed by their intensity.

Emotional maturity is not about suppressing or denying our feelings but rather about developing a healthy relationship with them. It involves recognizing that emotions are neither good nor bad, but simply information. By practicing emotional awareness, slowing down, and integrating our teachings of yoga, we can cultivate emotional maturity. This journey allows us to harness the wisdom within our feelings and make choices that align with our true selves.

Reach

THERE'S ALWAYS SOMEONE WILLING to reach out.

When life feels like a steady upstream battle, and you don't seem to be getting any closer to your goals, just remember this: you don't have to do it alone. You are surrounded by an intimate network of family, friends, and careers who have your back, as well as a broader network of colleagues, acquaintances, and role models, whose knowledge and expertise can benefit you.

You just have to ask.

Asking for help can be terrifying. To reach out to someone, you need to let go of something that was holding you steady. You might not have been going anywhere fast, but that handhold seemed like the only thing between you and drowning, and it was something you could control.

It was also holding you back from moving forward.

Yes, it might be a leap of faith to let go and reach out for someone else. It's scary to rely on others. It's scary to think that we can't do it all ourselves. It's uncomfortable to relinquish control. But if we want to fly, we have to let go of the fear of falling. We have to trust that there will be wind under our wings.

So, if you're feeling stuck — reach. Reach out and ask for help. Accept what support is offered. Let go of the fear of dependence, fear of vulnerability, and fear of failure which are keeping you from soaring.

Help might not always appear in the ways you expect. It might be a literal hand, pulling you from deep waters. It might be an understanding shoulder to cry and vent on. It might be a new professional, social, or creative opportunity. It might be the sudden, uncomfortable realization that what you thought you wanted, isn't in fact what's best for you.

Help is there. You just have to ask.

Impermanence

WE OFTEN FIND 'CHANGE' a scary thing. Although we know that life is in constant flow and forward momentum, when we think of something coming in to change our routines and our habits, or threatening to change what we know and how we see the world, we can react with fear and negativity. We feel safe in the perceived permanence of our lives, believing that any suggestion of flux, impermanence, or transformation must necessarily be for the worst.

But the impermanence of things is what makes them most beautiful! Everything around us is always transforming — day to night, season to season, full moon to new moon; the oceans and the seas, the sand dunes in our deserts, the earth beneath our feet — everything shifts. Everything follows its flow. Our own bodies are always in motion: the very act of breathing is the transformation of oxygen into energy, and our movement is the transformation of thought into action!

Our lives are like a constantly evolving dance, from one emotion to another, through one song to another, or like a flowing, shifting yoga sequence, working our way from one state of mind to another, through one pose to another. Each new dance, each new pose, builds on the last but remains distinct. We see where we have come from, but where we are now is unique, and there's no telling where we'll end up! We can sit with the feelings of discomfort knowing that we will pass through them, and we must rejoice in the love and happiness which act like a true north, a cardinal direction to which we can always return no matter where our flow takes us.

Being able to enter that flow and respect where it takes us, having the awareness to honor ourselves wherever we are in our dance, is the key to finding peace and fulfillment. To be able to do this, we must accept that nothing can stay as it is. Stasis is unnatural. Like the Earth herself, we are always shifting from one season to another. Transformation and growth are what life is made of, after all!

Journeys around the Sun

WHEN WE THINK OF our lives as journeys around the Sun, it becomes clear to us that with every new passage, every new solstice, we are changed. The Sun never sees the same person twice. How wonderful it must be from the Sun's perspective, to see us continually evolving, to see us learning from past journeys and growing closer to ourselves.

Our past journeys are the ones that shaped us and brought us to where we are now. Through the ups and the downs, through the learning curves and the growth opportunities — all the blessings we opened our hearts to have led to this moment. It can be difficult sometimes to think of our past Selves with love, compassion, and gratitude, but the person who enabled you to be here, now, deserves celebrating! Everything that defined them helped them to transform into you. They are strong, imperfect, and beautiful, and they are loved.

With every new journey around the Sun, it's vital to keep these past journeys in mind to see how far you've come.

Give yourself the credit and acknowledge your victories! Celebrate yourself in this moment. You can see where you've come from, and even if you might not be able to clearly see where you're going, your core values and principles are steering you toward your goals. By staying trusting and grateful, you have made the most out of your journey. You are strong, imperfect, and beautiful, and you are loved.

Looking out into the rising Sun as a new journey begins, prepare for the lessons and blessings this revolution will bring. Keep your heart open and courageous so that you can be more receptive to the coming opportunities. As you step out into your new journey around the Sun, do so with confidence and optimism, knowing that you are strong, imperfect, and beautiful and that you are loved.

Open Door

WHEN ONE DOOR CLOSES, another door opens — we just have to be willing to see it.

When we are told 'No,' when a job opportunity falls through, a relationship ends or never even starts, or our funds don't allow us that holiday, that car, or that school, it feels like a door we've been walking towards confidently and hopefully has just been slammed in our faces, and there's nowhere else worth going. It feels like the world turned its back on us and shut us out. It might even feel like the world is out to get you.

You have two choices at this junction. You could stay where you are, pounding on the door, yelling in frustration and anger about what you feel you've been robbed of.

Or you could turn around.

Let's face it — you didn't really know what to expect behind that door, so why are you so attached to it? Why is that door better than any other door?

You could turn around and notice the other doors that are available to you. Maybe you hadn't noticed them before when you were so focused on that particular option, but the other doors are there, waiting for you to try them.

Some will open, some will not. Some will do so easily; some will require tenacity and persistence on your behalf. But they are there.

Trusting that there are plenty of doors we could try, knowing that those that open will work out for us, perhaps in unexpected ways, makes it easier to see a closed door in a positive light. A closed door is simply an opportunity to try something else, something new, something unexpected. To open our minds and shift out of our comfort zone. To switch up our perspective and remain receptive to our blessings.

Retreat

WE SPEND OUR DAYS giving of ourselves. We give to our friends and family, and we give to our colleagues and bosses. We put our emotional, physical, and mental energies into ensuring everything is running smoothly, remembering to arrange that dinner, get that lightbulb fixed, or meet that deadline.

How can we clarify what brings us purpose and joy when we're so focused on everyone and everything else? By living constantly outside ourselves, we can become disconnected from our truth and power.

Take a break to reconnect with your voice after dedicating so much energy to giving it to others. Spending quality time with yourself is vital to understanding your priorities, purpose, and goals and getting back in touch with your strengths and direction.

Whether you journal, meditate, read, dance, or do yoga, take that time to retreat into yourself. Retreat into all the parts of you that need Love and Light and give to yourself.

While it may sound counter-intuitive, you must first provide for yourself to give more powerfully and focusedly to others. Isn't that what flight attendants instruct us to do? Put your oxygen mask on first before helping others. Take care of Yourself before you care for others. What can you do for anyone else if you're scattered, exhausted, and confused?

It's okay to give to yourself.

The energy that you dedicate to you is never lost. It strengthens you as you shine into the world with purpose, meaning, and impact.

Retreat and surrender are the first steps to spiritual growth. It can only come from within.

Patience and Humility

THROUGHOUT LIFE'S RICH AND varied adventures, two lessons keep coming back to me time and time again. Whether it's through witnessing someone else's struggle or learning the lessons again through personal experience, I'm always reminded of the importance of Patience and Humility.

We can sometimes approach new challenges with impatience and pride, seeking immediate gratification, validating ourselves, and believing ourselves to be 'ready.' We aim high straight off the bat--- the most complex yoga postures, the steepest ski runs, the longest trails, the most intense meditations, the most intricate book, the heaviest weights.

No matter how ready we believe ourselves to be, Patience and Humility are never far behind, waiting to teach us, again and again, the lessons we forget.

You can only build high with solid foundations.

Aiming for the top without building up first can cause over-exertion, injury, burning out, and perceived failure. Reaching for the stars without grounding yourself can become such a terrifying, off-putting experience that regaining the trust and courage to start again feels impossible.

Humility teaches us that we are not above the baby steps, the build-up, the small beginnings — and this is okay.

Patience teaches us to see further than tomorrow, to know the value of taking our time, and to understand the nature of growth.

They are loving teachers who consistently reward us for returning to them, swallowing our pride, and returning to the basics, the foundations, and the beginning. The most valuable journeys we take are those through which we grow the most.

Pranayama
Pause

Ujjayi Pranayama

"Victorious Breath" or "Ocean Breath"

Ujjayi Pranayama is known for its ability to calm the mind and warm the body. It can help increase focus, relieve tension, and maintain healthy blood pressure when practiced correctly.

This technique is often used in various styles of yoga, especially in Ashtanga and Vinyasa. Here's how to do it:

1. Sit comfortably on a yoga mat or a chair with your feet flat on the floor and your spine erect.

2. Close your eyes and take a deep breath in and out through your nose.

3. Now, inhale deeply through your nostrils. As you do, constrict the muscles in the back of your throat as if you were whispering. This will result in a soothing sound, similar to the sound of the ocean.

4. Hold your breath for a few seconds.

5. As you exhale, continue to constrict the muscles in the back of your throat to keep the ocean sound going. The out-breath should be long and smooth.

6. Repeat this process for several minutes, focusing on the sound of your breath and keeping it smooth and even.

Part Two

Recognizing your Samskaras

IT CAN BE DIFFICULT to see the patterns that govern our lives. They surround us and are a part of the kaleidoscopic tunnel we walk through as we step out into the world. Some patterns strengthen us and pave the way for powerful forward momentum, but others weaken us, distancing us from our power and independence and making it difficult to maintain our forward motion.

The Sanskrit word *samskaras* refers to these patterns, these emotional habits that our lives revolve around. Whether positive or negative, we get the best view of our own personal samskaras when we take a step back. Removing ourselves from the immediate desire to react, watching our thoughts, studying our behavior, and asking difficult and uncomfortable questions: Why did I do/think/feel that? Have I done/thought/felt that before?

Noticing both the helpful and harmful patterns allows you greater control over the path you walk. When we recognize the strengthening habits, we already enact, it becomes easier to nurture and solidify them, so that we can gain even more from our natural tendencies.

Recognizing the patterns and emotional habits that are holding us down is also so empowering. These are the patterns that keep up going in circles, dragging us under as we furiously tread water, reaching for the sky. These are the samskaras that result in the same scars — over and over again.

As always, coming from the perspective of Love, understand where and why these patterns developed and what they were trying to protect you from. Be grateful for their intention but recognize that you don't need them anymore. You're not scared. You're ready to stride forward into your truth, into your purpose, into your potential.

Hit the reset button on those patterns and habits that have been pulling you down. Replace them with new patterns that build you up and bring you closer to the best version of yourself! Build on the patterns that have elevated you this far so that they can be the wind under your wings as you soar ever onwards.

Speaking to Ourselves

No one speaks to you as much as you do yourself. Our own voice, our own opinions, and our own feelings are the ones we are most familiar with and the ones we are most accustomed to hearing. This is why what we say to ourselves and how we speak to ourselves is so important.

Often, if you compare how you speak to your friends and treat yourself, you'll find that you have so much more space, patience, and compassion for others. You let them make mistakes, forgive them; you give them a safe space to feel their feelings; you have so much time for them.

But when it comes to you, you're so hard on yourself! You don't let yourself make mistakes, and you struggle to forgive or forget the ones you do make. You minimize your feelings so they won't take up too much space. You berate yourself when things don't go as planned.

Just think: if you could lift yourself up as high as you lift your loved ones, the sky would be the limit!

All it takes is for you to start treating yourself as a friend.

"It's okay. You made a mistake this time, but remember yesterday? You did so well! And the day before! Tomorrow, you'll do well again."

"You are enough. Let's list all the times you have been enough."

"Of course, you feel tired. Think of all the things you've been juggling! How can I help?"

"It's completely understandable that you feel sad. Lots of stuff has been going on for you these days."

Rewrite your self talk. When you hold yourself accountable with Love and Compassion and own all your achievements and positive qualities, you empower yourself to reach your true potential.

Collaboration

If you want to go fast, go alone. If you want to go far, go together — African proverb.

IT CAN BE TEMPTING to think we're better off alone. We're in control of our schedule, of our product, of our progress. We can check up on ourselves, hold ourselves accountable, and manage every single detail of the process. Whether in your work, in your personal life, or when trying to master a new skill, the first inclination is usually to 'go it alone.'

When you care about quality and what you're sending out into the world, delegation is nerve-wracking and collaboration daunting. It's terrifying to release a part of your process to someone else and intimidating to rely on a partner.

Ego also plays a part, of course — my way is the better way; my standards are the only standards; I'm the only one who can meet my standards.

Delegation and collaboration require flexibility and open-mindedness that Ego simply has no room for.

There's something else that powering on alone doesn't leave room for. Growth, influxes of fresh and unexpected ideas, devil's advocacy, and objective accountability all come with opening the windows of your heart and your goals, and they all improve your process and your product. But more importantly, opening yourself to working with others ushers in support, camaraderie, light-heartedness, loyalty, and so much more!

What powering on alone does leave room for is burn-out, exhaustion, life imbalance, plateauing, and feeling hopeless. For many, this becomes a wake-up call; an alarm bell signaling that the way they've been going about their process has stopped being beneficial to them and their work.

When you care about yourself and the quality of what you're sending out into the world, delegation is strategic and collaboration beautiful. It's daring to release a part of your process to someone else, and brave to rely on a partner. They are the vital steps you take to build on what you've achieved so far.

Anitya

TRUSTING IN IMPERMANENCE, ANITYA, is easier said than done. It's a way of life that takes practice, self-discipline, and willingness.

> *"This too shall pass, so I will feel it fully and without fear. This too shall pass, so I will make the best out of it while it's here. This too shall pass, so I will be grateful and aware in the moment. This too shall pass, so I will learn what I can from the experience."*

But sometimes, more than faith, trust, or willingness, it's a way of life that requires Patience. This too shall pass — but when?

When life is easy and sunny, Anitya is about being aware, mindful, and grateful in the moment, appreciating these Universal gifts. When life is challenging us, Anitya is about Patience, or *Dhriti*: to persevere, and to hope. Embracing

Impermanence means the mindful practice of hope and growth in adversity, knowing that 'adversity' is simply a lesson we can learn from if we are able to sit through it.

We will unquestionably go through trying times, but Anitya tells us that they will pass. We do not know what they will become, or how we will react to them, but we know that these days will ebb, and new days will flow. All we must do is stay patient and live fully in the now, without longing for an imagined future or creating expectations for the times to come.

Dhriti shows us that good things come to those who can wait, persevere, to endure through the challenges and the lessons. To learn and to grow. To keep faith.

So let us stay patient and hopeful as we make the best of what life has to offer us.

Flexibility

IT MIGHT SOUND OBVIOUS if I say that flexibility is important in yoga. But I don't mean flexibility of the body — I mean flexibility of the Spirit. Yoga is a powerful teacher of the balance between freedom and restraint: the freedom that comes with learning to connect with ourselves; the restraint that comes from existing in a complex physical world. Finding and keeping that balance, dancing between total release and self-awareness, requires the flexibility to be constantly conscious of ourselves and adaptable to our rhythms.

The freedoms that yoga brings are so powerful — open muscles, deep nourishing breaths, oneness, and connection. But any restrictions that come from our physical bodies are also felt powerfully. Whether it's an injury from which we're recovering, a body that is larger or tighter than we would like, or a physical condition that presents additional challenges — all of these factor deeply into our yoga practice.

In many ways, life is similar to yoga. We're constantly spinning between working powerfully towards our intentions and dealing with limitations and constraints.

It's easy to slip into frustration, impatience, and pessimism when something is holding us back, but the best way to work with constraints is through loving compassion and space. Give yourself the space to heal, to grow, and to overcome challenges at your own pace. Give yourself the space to feel all those feelings that come to the surface, but don't let them tempt you into pushing yourself.

To give yourself this space, you might need to adapt your plan, modify your routine, or shift your perspective. You'll need to stay flexible and receptive, open to change and transformation. By doing this, you're not compromising your intentions or failing in your goals. Not at all! You're simply giving yourself the best tools to achieve your uniquely personal definition of success.

Vulnerability

WHAT DOES IT MEAN to be vulnerable?

It starts with authenticity. Being authentically yourself means standing in your truth, your power, your values, and your ideas, and expressing them honestly. Vulnerability is simply the next step: being authentically yourself around others; and expressing your feelings, truths, and ideas openly in public.

This is terrifying! It's where we run the risk of rejection, mockery, exclusion — all the things that threaten our need to belong, our need for community, our need for Tribe. Being vulnerable is one of the bravest things we can do, and so often, it ends up being the most rewarding.

There's a key ingredient to healthy, brave authenticity and vulnerability, though: Compassion.

Express yourself from the heart and lead with Love: Love for yourself, and Love for others. When your truth is rooted in self-love, you're safe from rejection and exclusion, and mockery can't hurt you. When your truth is rooted in love and compassion for others, similarity and difference are both as beautiful as each other and your vulnerability will empower those around you, whether they have a similar truth to you or come from a completely different perspective.

Being vulnerable is really about being honest, with yourself and with others. It's about showing up and being seen as you are, in all your complex beauty. It's about showing compassion and respect for the feelings, truths and ideas of those around you. Be fearlessly you so that others can be fearlessly them!

Next time you have an idea, don't hide behind someone else's! When you feel a certain way, express that emotion. If you have an opinion, share it. The world will be enriched and empowered by your contributions! And when someone else suggests an idea, expresses an emotion, or shares an opinion, let them know that you have been enriched and empowered by their contributions.

Root values

CHANGE, FLOW, AND TRANSFORMATION are all around us, and it's vital to accept and honor them so that we can make the best of where they take us. But it's equally essential that our roots be deep and powerful enough to keep our foundations strong so that we can go with the flow without losing or compromising ourselves, and without losing track of our intentions and goals.

Your roots are your connection to the Earth, to the Source. They ground you when life wants to run away with you. They are the stable foundation from which you can learn to fly. They are your magnetic North.

They grow from your values, the actions you take that align with them, the communities and Soul tribes that you develop based on them, and your ability to bring yourself back to them when you're feeling overwhelmed, tugged in all sorts of directions, or afraid. When you base your actions, decisions, and choices on your root values, you strengthen your connection with yourself and with the Earth, which gives you everything you need to thrive.

The best way to picture it is to visualize yourself as a strong tree, in its prime, full of vitality. Before you were able to grow tall, reaching for the stars, you grew down into the Earth, connecting powerfully with your Source. And as you grew taller and taller, and blossomed with beautiful flowers and fruits, your roots also grew deeper and deeper. Today, as you continue to reach for the stars, to blossom and bloom, your roots also must continue to evolve and be nurtured, so that they can empower you to grow stronger.

When you take time to regularly reconnect with your root values, you are grounding yourself so that you can grow. Strengthening the connection with yourself and with the Earth empowers you to reach new heights, so don't be afraid to fly!

Your Success

IN THE RUSH TO be productive, to self-improve, to 'make the best of a tough situation,' it can be easy to get lost in the whirlwind of tasks, self-imposed structures, and inward or outward pressure. But if we want to stay grounded and positive during times of change, when our usual parameters for Success are no longer applicable, it's just as important, if not more so, to give to ourselves and not only of ourselves, to dedicate time and energy to internal wellbeing as well as external pursuits.

I want to start off by saying that you're doing so well. You're here; you're functioning; you're alive — that's Success!

Giving to ourselves and nurturing our emotional and mental well-being, starts with comparing ourselves to who we were yesterday, not to whom others are today. Allow yourself to exist on your own terms, and don't let anyone else dictate how you should be feeling about yourself. And then remember to treat yourself kindly, to be compassionate towards yourself. The world has completely changed around you, and the rules are being re-made as we go. You're coping. That's amazing.

When you plan your day, make sure you include a moment for you. A moment to reconnect with yourself. A moment to remember how accomplished, talented and magical you are.

Maybe you'll meditate or spend some time sketching. Maybe you'll re-read your favorite book or write a poem or short story. Maybe you'll have a bath and nurture your body. Maybe you'll do some yoga or sit in the sun and bask. Whatever it is, it should be something that replenishes you and leaves you feeling content and optimistic. This is the energy that will flow through you, the energy you communicate to your loved ones. This is why giving to yourself is the best thing you can do for you, and those around you.

Un-learning

LOOKING BACK ON HISTORY it's clear to see that change doesn't happen smoothly or all at once. It's a painful, uncomfortable process full of friction, anger, momentum and hope. It's a gradual, inconsistent process full of stops and starts, first waves and second waves, while the status quo gets renegotiated. There's rarely a clear destination or blueprint.

Looking back on history, it's also clear to see that change is inevitable. Social and political structures are cyclically shaken to their core and re-built; nothing is allowed to stagnate or last forever.

In many ways, as a society, we have become so much more aware of the importance of change. I feel that resistance to change is gradually losing its grip, giving way to more acceptance and release.

We want to change. We want to make history so that the next decade is different from the one that came before. We want to be part of the momentum rather than the friction.

Being part of the momentum of change and transformation requires a lot from us. It requires a willingness to unlearn and learn. It requires consistency and discipline in educating ourselves and applying our knowledge. It requires a deep, reflective practice where we look back to see how to move forward — and how not to.

We must build new perspectives into habits and new habits into social norms. We must be willing to have the rug pulled from under our feet so that we can weave together a new rug, a better rug. One which brings us closer to a world where equality really means equality and diversity is celebrated in the rich tapestry of life.

Change and Growth

IT'S NATURAL FOR OUR minds to cling to the known, to the familiar, to those things that we can handle, whether they're good for us or not. It feeds our ego when we see around us a world that reflects what we know. To see a world that reflects what we don't know — now that would be terrifying, and exactly what we need in order to grow.

Distancing ourselves from our Ego, it becomes easier to see the patterns that we hold on to which work against our best interests. It also becomes easier to welcome the changes, the ebbs and flows which are a natural element of life.

By dismantling the Ego, we leave more room for our Self. The Self understands and welcomes the impermanence of things, and therefore has no expectation or attachment to specific outcomes and situations. The Self knows, on a level of deep consciousness, that all things change, and therefore that any phase, whether good or bad, will flow into a different phase.

The faith in impermanence empowers us to feel all our transient human emotions deeply, to truly experience the vast range of feelings humans are capable of, whether that be grief, fear, love, joy, sadness, boredom, jealousy, excitement, anticipation — but without letting the emotions become our masters. When we know that all things change, we can fearlessly dive into the emotions, through the emotions, and observe them, experience them, witness them, accept them, and watch them float away.

Things around us are changing all the time. The saying goes that you never step into the same river twice, but I believe it's truer to say that you never step into the same day twice. It may seem obvious, but reminding ourselves that change is not only natural but an essential force of growth can make every day, every week, every month more magical and mindful.

Pranayama
Pause

Kapalabhati Pranayama

"SKULL SHINING BREATH"

KAPALABHATI IS AN INVIGORATING and warming breath practice that should be done with caution. If you have any medical conditions such as high blood pressure, heart disease, or a hernia, or if you're pregnant, you should avoid this practice.

This breathing technique internally tones and cleanses the respiratory system of toxins. At the same time, it is known for its ability to energize the body and clarify the mind. Here's how to do it:

1. Sit comfortably on a yoga mat or on a chair with your feet flat on the floor with your spine erect.

2. Place your hands on your knees, palms open to the sky.

3. Take a deep breath in.

4. As you exhale, pull in your stomach. Pull your navel in back towards the spine. Do as much as you comfortably can.

You may keep your right hand on the stomach to feel the abdominal muscles contract. Pull the navel in.

5. As you relax the navel and abdomen, the breath flows into your lungs automatically.

6. Now repeat this but inhale quickly then exhale quickly as if you are churning the breath from your belly. Take 20 such breaths to complete one round of Kapalabhati pranayama.

7. After completing the round, relax with your eyes closed and observe the sensations in your body.

8. Try two more rounds.

Part Three

Compassion

A GROWTH MINDSET IS the most valuable tool we can mobilize, both as individuals and as a society. It's what enables honest reflection, authentic dialogue, genuine transformation, and sustainable change. A growth mindset is our ability to transform ourselves and our communities into representations of our core values. It's our greatest superpower!

That's not to say that it's easy, though. To grow, we must be able to honestly look back at where we've come from, and we must be able to fearlessly and compassionately name our ugly bits, our mistakes, our faults, and our flaws. This way, they give us the power to transform, rather than us giving them the power to hold us back.

Even more terrifying, we must be open to how others perceive our behaviors, how others are impacted by us, and what our peers see in us that we might be blind to. Listening with an open heart; accepting others and ourselves; giving ourselves the permission to be 'not-perfect' so that we create the space to grow into who we want to become. This is the basis of the authentic dialogue between us and the world that is going to help us transform.

The key, as always, lies in the Ego. The Ego has no compassion, it only condemns. So, if it were to truly listen, it would have to turn its condemnation onto itself, and that would be unacceptable. To prevent this, it gets defensive and angry, fogging up the mirror so we can preserve the flattering view of ourselves.

To let go of the Ego is to let go of condemnation. It is to embrace Compassion, for others and for ourselves. And once we have Compassion for ourselves, for the influences that made us, for our flaws, mistakes and ugly bits, then we can truly look at them, name them, and transform them.

Resilience

RESILIENCE IS HAVING THE emotional tools to receive all the depth and range of transient human experiences, without losing touch with our perspectives or core grounding values. These tools, which include hope, mindfulness, self-awareness, self-compassion, faith, determination, willpower, and far-sightedness, to name just a few, are muscles that can be trained by conscious choices and decisions. Every day, we can actively choose to become more resilient in the face of challenges, thereby empowering ourselves to be in flow with what the world has to offer.

Resilience works on a personal level, helping us as individuals to stay rooted and grounded through the storms, but it also functions on a societal level. Societies can be easily threatened, destabilized, or torn apart, or they can be resilient in the face of physical and social challenges. Of course, much of societal resilience depends on access to food, water, education, and employment, but it also relies heavily on its parts.

Resilient societies are built by people who are grounded enough to take change and difficulty in their stride, without turning against each other. Resilient societies are built by people who widen their perspectives to consider the experiences of others, so that they play positive roles in them. Resilient societies are built by people who can look honestly at themselves, and work to make themselves better.

Resilient societies are built by resilient people. And resilient people are built with compassion and hope.

So let us, as a society, flex the muscles of compassion and hope as we navigate the lessons that Life is offering us.

Sankalpa

WITH EVERY DAWNING OF a new year, people are often drawn to resolutions, goals, and other measures of success or validation. These tend to address elements we feel are lacking in our lives, ways in which we fall short of some criteria, or external stimulants that will make us happy. Most are ego-driven and fizzle out after a few weeks because they do not address our need for connection to ourselves.

There is much to say for setting new goals, but there would be so much more to say for starting new journeys. I encourage you to get brave and experimental with your new Selves, to start journeys, to affirm your aliveness in the present moment, and to harmonize your mind and body, not in a goal, not in a resolution, but in a *Sankalpa*.

A Sankalpa is an intention, formed in that sweet spot between the heart and mind. It's a refinement and a focus of willpower, both psychological and spiritual. It is a vow, an expression of resolve, an embodiment of will. It's your Highest Self drawing you towards yourself.

The practice of Sankalpa — from *San*, connection to the highest truth, and *Kalpa*, a profound vow — is based on the premise that you already are who you need to be. All you need to do is focus your mind, connect to your heart, and channel the divine. Your true nature exists, you only need to unite with it.

In each yoga practice, most teachers, including myself, ask students to create an intention for their practice. Our Sankalpa reminds us always why we are here, and connects us to our purpose, or our *dharma*. Applying this philosophy outside our yoga practice empowers us to live with intentionality and purpose, and to always come back to our union with the divine.

A Game of Blame

THERE'S A GAME THAT people seem to enjoy playing. It's a game that means they don't have to face reality, adapt to situations, or take responsibility for their own lives. It's a game that allows people to cling to their image of themselves and of what 'normal' should be.

It's the Blame Game.

The Blame Game becomes a bit of a national sport in times of crisis. People always find someone, other than themselves, who must be actively responsible for a situation. This way, they can sit in righteous anger and refuse to see a crisis from different perspectives. They can remain blind to the lessons to be learned. They can ignore their own role in creating or aggravating the issue. Because it's clearly someone else's fault.

The Blame Game is the easy, reassuring road. In times of crisis, it's so simple to shift our gaze outwards and blame others, usually completely irrationally. It means we don't have to examine ourselves and our priorities with a critical eye.

Love, Kindness, and Compassion are the difficult paths, the rewarding paths, the healing paths. When our sense of 'normal' is threatened, this is the path that refuses to succumb to fear and anger. It's the path that sees the suffering of others and wants to make it better. It's the path that sees that we're all in this together and we're stronger as One. It's the path that expands our perspective so that we can act for the greater good.

In times of crisis, Love and Kindness are what will help us create a better, more united, more diverse tomorrow.

True Balance

It can sometimes seem like the balance of our emotional well-being hangs on a knife edge, and all it takes is a nudge to make us feel like we need to start over. We're scared of stumbling back into negative thought patterns and feeling spirals, so it's tempting to protect ourselves from these 'nudges' by limiting our exposure to stressors.

In times of crisis and social upheaval, though, these 'nudges' often come in the form of news, awareness, and educating oneself about what's going on around us.

So where is that fine line? The balance between 'the news just depresses me' and 'it's important to stay aware and educated so we can address the issues of our time'?

That fine line starts with our own definition of 'balance.' Often, we mistake 'balance' for 'feeling full of love and gratitude all the time.' But one of the most transcendental aspects of the human experience is those emotions that signal to us that something isn't right: sadness, anger, fear. Without these powerful emotions, inner work and self-improvement would be impossible; they are the catalysts that wake us up and inspire change.

'Balance' is being in the flow of emotions, experiencing them fully, and letting them go. It's being able to return to love and gratitude after experiencing anger or sadness. Most importantly, it's trusting your ability to do so. Only when you have faith in impermanence and your ability to re-center yourself will you be empowered to feel all your transient human emotions fully and freely.

So, educate yourself and read the news, but don't flood yourself with stressful stimuli. Feel the anger, fear, and hurt fully — they are justified — but don't wallow in them.

Be compassionate with yourself when you're feeling low and love yourself back to the Light. Anger may inspire change, but Love will cement it.

Expectations

LET'S DIVE INTO THE most significant reason people struggle to find balance amidst ambiguity: our own expectations.

Uncertainty comes from being unsure whether our expectations will be met, and then finding, more often than not, that they won't be. Our feelings of bewilderment, panic, and lack of control, on the other hand, come from how attached we become to those expectations. When we grow attached to a specific outcome, it's no wonder we're thrown off balance if things turn out differently!

That's not to say that you mustn't feel positive about something, or look forward to an event, or hope that something happens a certain way. It just means that the heart of your positivity, optimism, and hope must be rooted within you. While external events can enhance these mindsets, they cannot take them from you.

Hoping that your actions yield certain results is very different than expecting them to.

Hope is an innate spiritual muscle; it's within us. No one can take it from us. Expectation, on the contrary, demands that external factors meet us halfway. When Hope isn't met, we re-center and grow. When Expectation isn't met, we're stumped and angry.

Releasing our attachment to expectations helps us stay afloat when things go a little crazy; it helps us coast along the currents of life, rather than struggle against them.

This isn't an easy thing to do. We're wired to work in a 'give and take,' 'action-reaction,' 'cause-and-consequence' kind of world, where our every action is measured according to the expected result. What are we going to get from this? But the key to maintaining balance through what feels like utter chaos is quite simple.

Act without expectation.

When we release our attachment to expectations, we become much more adaptable, much more centered, and, most importantly, we leave plenty of room for growth.

Transitions

LIFE IS ABOUT OUR ability to grow, to evolve, and to transform into our best selves. It's all about the journey! But it's not a smooth, flawless, continuous journey. It's a journey of phases, stop-starts, U-turns and lane changes. It's a journey of transitions between what we used to be, where we used to be, and the people we are becoming.

Transitions can be exciting, jarring, terrifying, challenging, and stimulating, or all of these at once! They impact our relationship with ourselves, with our family, and our friends, and they can impact our jobs, our sense of self-worth and purpose, and our perspectives on the world.

Sometimes transitions happen almost naturally, and we find ourselves drifting into a new lane until we have no choice but to embrace the change.

Sometimes they hit us in the face out of the blue, and we are presented with a sudden choice.

Sometimes they announce themselves with symptoms such as restlessness, discomfort, disconnect, and dissatisfaction, which don't go away until we turn around to face them and ask them what they're trying to tell us.

Sometimes, it's about giving the people around us the space to transform and grow, no matter how much it scares us. It can be tempting to try and keep those we love in a phase that we're comfortable with, but this inhibits their potential. When we love someone, we honor their transitions.

But transitions aren't just about moving from one to another. There's so much to learn from the spaces in between; from that strange, limbo-like place where one chapter is closing and another opening. We learn about ourselves, our feelings around transformation, and our relationships. We learn more about our values and priorities. We learn about the importance of our foundations in empowering us to take leaps of faith.

Right Knowledge

TO KNOW CLEARLY. TO go through life with clarity and vision. We all wish for it, because when we can't identify the truth of a situation, we often get hurt or disappointed.

The Sutras differentiate beautifully between these two states of being: proper *knowledge is built on perceiving the truth of a situation* (1.7), *and false knowledge is created by our misperceptions* (1.8). This false knowledge leads to pain and strife, conflict and misunderstanding, intolerance and hatred.

How can we achieve clarity? How can we find right knowledge? The Sutras tell us that "the source of right knowledge is built on clear sense perception, logic, and verbal communication." These are not elements that always come naturally to us. Our perceptions and logic are often clouded by past experiences, emotional reactions, and expectations, while authentic and honest communication can seem challenging and unpleasant.

Yet, if we want to avoid the pitfalls of false knowledge, it's vital that we find the ability to see each situation, person, or event as new. Examining it solely on its factors without interference from past patterns and expectations. When we can see it clearly for what it is, rather than what we assume or expect it to be, we can use logic to come closer to right knowledge. Precise communication empowers us to ask for any clarification or information we might need.

To perceive right knowledge, rather than our projection of the truth, we must be willing to communicate bravely. We can do this by being honest and authentic about our motivations and asking the questions we need to ask to better understand a situation. In this way, communication enables us to learn more about ourselves, the exact circumstances, and our interactions with the world around us. It's our best tool for finding the truth.

Clear communication can help us see beyond the filter of misperception, steering us away from hurt and pain to move forward in positivity and confidence.

Embracing Neutrality

THE BHAGAVAD GITA, A sacred Hindu scripture, offers profound insights into the importance of neutrality in our lives, especially when faced with conflicting opinions. This ancient text teaches us that neutrality is not about indifference or apathy but rather a state of equanimity that allows us to navigate life's challenges with grace and wisdom.

Neutrality, as depicted in the Bhagavad Gita, encourages us to rise above the sway of emotions, desires, and attachments, allowing us to make decisions from a place of clarity and wisdom.

The Bhagavad Gita presents the symbolic battle between Arjuna, the warrior, and his inner conflicts. Arjuna finds himself torn between his duty as a warrior and his compassion for his relatives on the opposing side. Lord Krishna, his charioteer and guide, advises him to embrace neutrality by detaching himself from the outcomes and focusing on performing his duty without attachment to the results.

The Bhagavad Gita teaches us that neutrality is not about avoiding action but performing our duties with a sense of detachment. It emphasizes the importance of acting selflessly without being swayed by personal desires or expectations. By cultivating this attitude, we can maintain our inner peace and remain unaffected by the ups and downs of life.

Detachment does not imply a lack of care or concern for others. Instead, it encourages us to let go of our ego-driven desires and attachments, allowing us to act in the best interest of all beings. By practicing detachment, we free ourselves from the burden of expectations and find liberation from the cycle of suffering.

The Bhagavad Gita teaches that neutrality is not just a means to navigate worldly challenges but also a path to self-realization. By embracing neutrality, we can transcend the limitations of our ego and connect with our higher self. This connection leads to a deeper understanding of our true nature and the realization that we are all interconnected.

Soul Tribe

ALONE, OUR VOICES AND actions can sometimes feel small and inconsequential. Whether we're trying to communicate to ourselves or others, make a change in our lives, or bring new perspectives to our communities, growth and improvement are difficult especially if we're trying to grow ourselves out of a tough spot.

It's a journey that shouldn't be taken alone.

If we keep using our voices and actions to express our authentic truths compassionately, despite feeling small, despite feeling powerless, we make way for something truly magical. We create something powerful. We become magnetic.

By quietly, persistently, and bravely taking even the smallest steps along the journey you know you need to take, you attract those who have walked, are walking, or will walk a similar path into your life. People who will help lift you and people whom you will help. People who understand on a level you couldn't even imagine.

When you own your truth, you become magnetic to your Soul Tribe. And their voices and actions will be joined with yours until that quiet voice you thought was powerless to make change has become the mightiest roar.

The foundations you build with your Soul Tribe are a lifelong building block. They strengthen you and those around you to create a life that meets your deepest needs and values. They empower you to adapt and thrive, to rise above challenges, and spread your wings.

Only by being true to yourself can you attract your Soul Tribe. Most importantly, by staying true to yourself despite your doubts and fears, you empower yourself to draw up healthy boundaries in your life. This will protect you from those who would detract from your journey and ensure that the people in your life are indeed part of your Tribe.

Together, you can fly.

Pranayama
Pause

Bhramari Pranayama

"BEE BREATH"

BHRAMARI PRANAYAMA IS KNOWN to relieve tension, anger, and anxiety instantly. It is a very effective breathing technique for people suffering from hypertension as it calms down the agitated mind.

This technique is known for its calming effects, reducing stress and anxiety. Here's how to do it:

1. Sit comfortably on a yoga mat or a chair with your feet flat on the floor and your spine erect.

2. Place your index fingers on your ears. There is a cartilage between your cheek and ear. Place your index fingers on the cartilage.

3. Take a deep breath in, and as you breathe out, gently press the cartilage. You can keep the cartilage pressed or press it in and out with your fingers while making a loud humming sound like a bee.

4. You can also make a low-pitched sound similar to "Om," but it is a good idea to make a high-pitched one for better results.

5. Breathe in again and continue the pattern 3-4 times.

Part Four

So Ham

CARVING OUT TIME TO be with ourselves can be difficult. The realities and challenges of our daily lives, let alone the momentous changes sweeping across the world right now, are never far from our thoughts. Being in the present moment is hard. Feeling a connection sometimes seems impossible.

Mantras are a powerful vehicle for uniting the mind and body in focus. Bringing the two together magnifies our will and amplifies the impact of our me-time, sending it rippling through our mind, nervous system, breath, and muscles right down to our bones. Mantras empower us to forge a protective channel for our focus, safe from the world's distractions.

You don't necessarily need to sit down and meditate to allow the magic of mantras into your life. You can weave them seamlessly into the fabric of your day. Driving or walking, cooking, cleaning or showering, those first five minutes after the alarm goes off: all these moments can be made immeasurably richer by the silent repetition of a mantra.

Lately, I've been meditating on the mantra "*So Ham.*" This mantra has been used for thousands of years. It is one of the first to be taught to beginner practitioners — not because it is less powerful or impactful than others, but because it is so fundamental to Connection, Oneness, Being One With All That Is. It's the answer to the central question, *Koham*, Who Am I?

So Ham: I am That.

It mirrors the sound of our breath as we inhale and exhale, connecting our waking minds to our bodies. It reminds us of our divine connection with the Universe, with Energy, with all of Creation, helping us feel held and supported. It brings us intensely back to ourselves, our bodies, our moment, our existence. It is both within us and all around us. We exist within it, and we are one with it.

Inner Child

IT'S SO DIFFICULT TO genuinely press pause. When life is going full swing, there's never an easy way to prioritize stillness, and when stillness is forced upon us, taking a genuine break is still somehow tricky.

Even in the name of stillness and spiritual growth, we tend to overload our minds with 'things to do.' Meditate, journal, do yoga, hang out with your Soul Tribe, read a new book, learn something new, research 'how to Surrender,' join a forum to ensure we're doing it right...

Where is the genuine pause here? Where is our time to safely, peacefully, and compassionately let our brains assimilate and process? We need a space for our mind to breathe while doing something that brings us joy, simply for the sake of it.

Occasionally, pressing pause on our drive to grow, achieve, and self-improve is the most valuable step in that direction. We need to give ourselves room to BE; a safe space where it's okay not to fly forward at the speed of light in pursuit of our goals.

These moments allow us to reconnect to our core grounding values and joys. Amid all the busyness, or all the spiritual journeying, bring yourself back to the basics.

What did you love doing as a kid? What brought the biggest smile to your face?

Did you love rolling down hills? Jumping on the trampoline? Fingerpainting? Climbing trees? Reading fiction, fantasy, or fairy tales? Playing with dolls? Exploring your street on your bike?

Whatever it was, and even if you've not experienced it in years, give yourself that space. Reconnect with your inner child and feel unadulterated joy simply for the sake of it.

Bravery

PEOPLE OFTEN MISTAKE THE absence of fear for bravery. And people often limit their definition of bravery to intense, one-off, self-sacrificing, or just insane experiences.

But bravery is a mindset and a habit. It's a muscle that you can train, just like hope. It's a practice you can get intentional about, so it's a constant in your life, not a one-off. And most importantly, bravery is showing up even when you're scared. It's not the absence of fear. It's being willing to stay true to your authentic self in the face of your fear.

Bravery can be speaking your truth when uncomfortable with it and its consequences. Bravery can be staying true to your feelings and instincts when your ego or peers are trying to sway you. It can be asking the questions you don't want the answer to or asking the uncomfortable questions to which you need the answer.

Bravery is listening compassionately to criticism and being open to new perspectives, even on ourselves. It's being willing to see what is familiar in a new light.

It's facing reality without being dominated by it and honoring our aspirations without being controlled by them. It's being ready to try new things and withhold judgment on them.

In many senses, bravery is all wrapped into honesty, openness, realism, and idealism. And, like most things, it's not an easy habit to develop. The warm cocoon of comfort zones, the safety of being perceived as likable and successful, the comfort of blaming others for our shortcomings and theirs, the easy company of bitterness and resentment — all these influences make bravery a scary, difficult choice. They make bravery a courageous choice.

But it's a choice we can all make.

'Schadenfreude'

'SCHADENFREUDE,' THE PLEASURE DERIVED from another person's misfortune, is an entirely human, natural emotion. Especially if it concerns a person by whom we have felt victimized, betrayed, and misrepresented. It should also be an emotion that slightly shakes us up, though.

It alerts us to the power we've given this person over our spiritual landscape. It signals that we've allowed something to pull us away from Compassion. We've let the Shadow out to play.

Everyone has a Shadow. There's no shame in the Shadow. It's simply important to recognize the feelings that come from the Shadow-place and to understand what their purpose is.

Schadenfreude is a Shadow-emotion. It's petty, vindictive, and self-gratifying. It's there to boost our Ego and make us feel good in a cheap, easy way. It exists in the Shadows of our subconscious and pokes its head out when our defenses are down.

As I said, this is natural and very human. We are messy, imperfect, raw, and beautiful creatures. The idea of the Shadow is not to shame ourselves, repress our feelings, and judge ourselves harshly. It's just about awareness.

Like most Shadow feelings, Schadenfreude is about our Shadows trying to protect us and make us feel good. It means something, or someone has shaken up our spiritual landscape and poked at our vulnerabilities. It's a knee-jerk reaction to a situation we've felt attacked by

When we feel a Shadow-emotion rise to the surface, the first thing to do is thank our Shadows. They are just trying to protect us, and in so doing, they have alerted us that we're a little off-balance and lost our grounding.

Thank your Shadow, accept the emotion, and accept that warning. Take the necessary steps to re-center yourself, find your grounding, and return to Compassion.

No one has the power to pull you entirely away from Compassion except for you.

Intentionality

EVERYTHING WE DO, EVERY act, process, or journey we commit to, we must approach with Intentionality.

Without Intentionality, it becomes difficult to assemble into coherent growth the bits and bobs that make up our often-messy journeys.

What do I mean by Intentionality? I mean knowing where you'd like to be heading. Not in the sense of exact, inflexible goals. More in knowing the Intention, or Sankulpa in Sanskrit, behind each act.

"I know the relationship I want to have with myself. I know how I want to feel about my job. I know the relationship I want to have with my finances. I know the impact I would like to have on my community."

And I know the small steps I need to take to help me along these journeys.

Approaching your life with Intentionality means that all the small things you do — healthy choices, managing your spending, the daily grind — take on extra power and meaning. You KNOW why you're doing them. You KNOW where they can take you.

There are some small but impactful rituals you can adopt to imbue your actions with meaning and bring yourself back to Intentionality.

Values Check-Up

- Choose five values you want to be the defining features of your life (for example, compassion, growth, creativity, generosity, honesty, discovery, justice, accountability, independence...).

- Once a day or once a week, run through how you've aligned with these values.

- When faced with a choice or decision, refer to these values to act as your guide.

- Create a mantra from them that you can use whenever you need.

- Get creative! Make little cards that you can place around the house so you're constantly reminded of who you want to be.

Start with a Sankulpa

Start every day with a breathing session, as short as five minutes if you're rushed, during which you focus on your Intention. This could be an Intention for this month, this day, this year---whatever you feel comfortable with!

Before you start any project or perform any action, take a breath and speak your Intention to yourself. Remind yourself of the relationship between your actions and your Intention.

Viparyaya

ONE OF THE MANY challenges within a deep self-study practice is the trap of viparyaya, or the state of misperception. Sanskrit for 'reversed' or 'loss of consciousness,' viparyaya refers to wrong knowledge stemming from incorrect thoughts, assumptions, or perceptions, often based on cultural or personal biases and misunderstandings. It can lead to 'impurities' of the mind, such as fear, hate, attachment, or ignorance, and it clouds our perception when we're simply trying to observe our truths.

Self-study aims to perceive through pramana, or a 'source of right knowledge,' so that we can see ourselves accurately and honestly, without judgment or fear, and 'become established in our own True Nature' (Sutra 1.3).

But how can we become more aware of the source of our self-knowledge? How can we distinguish between false assumptions, distorted perception, and genuine insight?

The arduous but rewarding journey of self-discovery requires that we cultivate a willingness to become curious, to question our assumptions, to seek the aperture of perception, and to see clearly. We will need to observe and watch our minds, to understand how our thoughts flow and form and then develop the discipline to still them.

Patanjali speaks of five vrittis or fluctuations of the mind. Pramana is the first, the source of right knowledge, but viparyaya is the second, followed by vikalpa (verbal delusion, imagination, fanciful understanding), nidrā (sleep, dullness of mind), and smṛiti (memory, unquestioning acceptance) (Sutra 1.6).

Our mental activities can be categorized within these five fluctuations. By observing and challenging our thoughts, we can identify which vritti our self-knowledge is based in and, therefore, whether it is a true insight or a false perception.

When you become intimate with the patterns of your mind, you can begin a practice that embodies the true essence of yoga. Sutra 1.2 states that yoga restricts *the fluctuations of the mind.* It's the art of finding stillness in true knowledge. It's the essential step towards Sutra 1.3: to become established in your own True Nature.

Grief and Gratitude

"Grief and Gratitude don't cancel each other out. They sit side by side." - Megan Devine.

WE TALK ABOUT GRATITUDE a lot. As a way of staying connected to ourselves and the Universe. As a pathway to inner calm and purpose. As a daily practice to infuse our lives with intentionality. We are often reminded to lean into what we are thankful for and feel humbled, grateful, and loving.

I walk my talk and try to practice Gratitude every day, just as I guide others to do. But a practice that can be difficult and moving at the best of times is even more challenging when we sometimes fear for all that we were grateful for or maybe when it can be difficult to live our best lives.

This is where we confront the myth that Gratitude is a magic band-aid that makes all the pain disappear. Where we stand in the discomfort of knowing that Gratitude is not a shortcut to eternal joy, nor does it only co-exist with happiness.

Gratitude is not about canceling out the sorrow. It's not about self-medicating with positivity and 'not feeling' the sadness.

Gratitude exists side-by-side with sorrow. It takes sorrow's hand and helps us feel it fully, experience it authentically, and move through it. It keeps us in mind of the impermanence of suffering while we flow with its currents.

Gratitude reminds us that grace co-exists with sorrow. We can fully experience pain, sadness, anger, and grief even while feeling grateful for the beauty that lives alongside it.

Listening

As a species, we tend to talk more than we listen. This means our conversations inevitably veer towards a monologue rather than a dialogue, and our voices are used to entrench us into the perspectives we know rather than as a tool to help us grow. When we talk but don't listen, there's no space for growth and no space for our Higher Selves.

To me, that's not what communicating is about. Our throat chakra, Vishuddha, is about our voices, our truth, and our power to express it. But it's also about our power to make space for the truth of others, our power to listen, and our power to honor the voices of those around us.

This means it's about compassion and courage to be heard and listen openly.

Sometimes listening takes work. Sometimes, it's actively uncomfortable. Sometimes, talking feels more gratifying. Sometimes, we talk because we feel heard, and sometimes we talk because we don't feel heard. Often, we listen only to answer.

But have we learned to truly listen?

Let our Vishuddha Chakra be as open as ever, flexing the listening muscles we've been neglecting.

Remember the power and meaning of your heart in conversation. Remember that sometimes your voice is more impactful when it is not used. Remember how much you can learn when you truly hear and respect others.

Hope

DOES IT SOMETIMES FEEL like you can't catch a break?

You can take a few steps to help yourself — and the first is to love yourself. Yes, you may feel fear, pessimism, anger, hatred, or hurt; these are feelings you are often told are unhelpful, inappropriate, or selfish.

But I don't believe that.

These intense feelings are reactions to our boundaries being pushed. They are signals that something is clashing with our values or that we are engaging with the world in ways that hurt us.

So take a moment to be grateful for these signals, for your body telling you something isn't right. Thank the anger, the hurt, and the fear for letting you know that something needs to change. Love the parts of you that scream for something different and tell them that you hear them. Give them the grace and space to express themselves. And then let them go.

Ground yourself in your core values and priorities. Come back to them when you feel yourself slipping down a rabbit hole and know that as long as you base your choices and actions on these values, you will be okay no matter what happens. They are the roots that center you and help you weather the storms.

Most importantly, train and flex that hope muscle. A well-developed hope habit will get you through most things.

Mindfulness

IT'S EASY TO BECOME caught up in our heads, with thoughts flying left, right, and center, things to achieve, pressures to respond to, and people to think of. This very human tendency to live not in the here and now but in the imaginary future, or the present that is beyond our control, can significantly increase our stress, anxiety, and general un-wellness.

Mindfulness has been a buzzword for many years, and I stand by it. But the word itself can be misleading. In many ways, mindfulness brings ourselves out of our minds, our heads, and back into our bodies — back into the part of us that physically viscerally experiences the here and the now. And while it isn't necessarily easy, mindfulness is beautifully simple.

An excellent way to start training ourselves to be mindful is to name thoughts and feelings as they arise:

Oh, there's that thought about how I'll never please my boss. I wonder what triggered it this time?

Oh, there's anxiety. I can feel it in my chest. I wonder what triggered it this time?

Transforming five minutes of the day into an opportunity to reconnect with our bodies is also infinitely powerful.

How is my physical body experiencing the world at this very moment?

What are my senses receiving?

The central element of mindfulness is the absence of judgment. We let ourselves become fully aware of the present moment, of what is happening inside and outside of ourselves, but we do not judge it. It helps us grow more in tune with what's happening, what we're doing, and the space we're evolving in without being carried away and overwhelmed by our sometimes turbulent inner and outer landscapes.

It's a tool for developing our resilience and empowers us to make the most out of the lives we are offered.

Pranayama
Pause

Sitali Pranayama

"COOLING BREATH"

SITALI PRANAYAMA CAN HELP to cool the body, reduce stress and anxiety, and improve focus and concentration. It's also said to help with conditions such as indigestion and ulcers.

This technique is known for its cooling effects and is especially beneficial during hot weather or after a heated yoga practice. Here's how to do it:

1. Sit comfortably on a yoga mat or a chair with your feet flat on the floor and your spine erect.

2. Close your eyes and take a few deep breaths to center yourself.

3. Stick out your tongue and curl the sides of the tongue upward towards the center to form a tube. If you can't curl your tongue, purse your lips to create an "O" shape like you are sipping through a straw.

4. Inhale deeply through the tube or "O" shape you've created with your tongue or lips. You should feel the cool air passing over your tongue or through your lips as you breathe in.

5. Close your mouth and exhale slowly through your nose.

6. Repeat this process for several minutes, focusing on the cooling sensation of the breath.

Part Five

Discipline

MANY OF US MIGHT shudder when we hear the word 'discipline.' It's a word that is sadly associated with depriving ourselves, forcing ourselves, or being punished. This makes it difficult for us to truly engage and resonate with self-discipline as we pursue our growth journeys. But Discipline is really the ultimate reward mechanism, the ultimate act of self-pleasure.

I want to transform the negative associations of Discipline because Discipline is the greatest gift you can give yourself. Self-discipline is the most extraordinary form of self-love.

Let's start with what Discipline is not:

It's not about accomplishments.

It's not about achieving.

It's not about self-punishment or self-loathing

To be sustainable and effective, Discipline must be rooted in self-love. 'I am giving this to myself because I am worthy.' 'I am practicing this because I love myself.' 'I am disciplined in this regard because it helps me grow closer to my Highest Self.'

In this way, Discipline has less to do with accomplishment and more with intention and commitment. When we commit to our intention, and when we are intentional in our commitments, Discipline is our gift to ourselves.

Our yoga practice's very act of Practice is Discipline in action. Yoga teaches us to continually keep turning the wheels we set in motion, whether we need to modify our practice to fit into today's schedule or suit our body's needs. We are continually working on our growth journey from a place of grace and love.

As with everything, the lessons we learn on the mat empower us daily. The grace and love that our self-discipline is rooted in become the foundations for our growth, from transforming our eating habits, our work-life balance, or our thought patterns to becoming the person the Universe calls us to be.

Simplicity

WHEN I FIND MYSELF getting overwhelmed, there's one core value I try to return to, like a magnet to true North: Simplicity.

To flow with life, creating the smallest amount of friction and resistance possible, I like to think of myself as a radiant, streamlined being, unburdened by unnecessary baggage. This helps me shed what is causing my sense of being overwhelmed or my attachment to and anxiety about things that I cannot control.

Overwhelm comes from having, seeking, or doing too much. When we surround ourselves with material objects that fill our professional or personal schedules, we seek externally something we can only find within ourselves. We clutter our emotional and physical spaces, drowning out the whispers of Souls, clouding our core values, and stretching ourselves too thin.

It's important in these moments to remember that we are not our belongings, we are not our professions, we are not our social status. To re-center myself in my core values, I peel back the layers of clutter: the layer formed by my career and any friction arising there. I peel back the layer formed by the things I own. I peel back the layers of my relationships and keep peeling back layers until I am left with nothing but the Light at the core of myself.

Until I remember who I am.

When we have unwavering knowledge of ourselves, we become our own North Star. Its light, our light, can guide us to shed those elements of our life that do not directly serve our journey and to accept those elements that we cannot control without judgment and without anxiety.

Koshas

IN THE TAITTIRIYA UPANISHAD, we are described as having five layers of existence, known in Sanskrit as Koshas. This translates as 'sheaths' because the layers don't exist in isolation from each other. Each one slots into the next like a sword into a scabbard, creating strength in unity and oneness of purpose

One of the aims of yoga is to train our awareness of these sheaths, to understand which one we are inhabiting at any given time, to be able to flow through them and integrate them, and maybe eventually transcend beyond them.

The five koshas that make up your being flow from the most physical, most tangible sheath, your body, down to the vastest and most subtle inner bliss. They are interpenetrating and interconnected, each layer more subtle than the last and encompassing its denser layers. To reach a deep knowing of Self, it is vital to understand yourself within each Kosha and bring them together in balance.

Through the practice of yoga, we strive to move through each layer. We grow our awareness and our conscious control of the flow within and around us. This conscious knowledge helps us realize that we are multifaceted, unique beings distinguished from others on many levels yet intimately connected and divine. We are distinct, but never separate.

Koham? Who am I?

The answer is a complex one. Like us, the answer is multifaceted and distinct yet illustrative of the common divinity uniting us.

Yoga asks us to search for ourselves at every Kosha. Am I my physical body? Am I my vital energy? Am I my thoughts? Am I my inner knowing? Am I my Anandamaya, truth-wisdom-bliss?

Who am I at each Kosha, and how can I integrate them to become One with Myself?

Contract and Expand

DISCOMFORT, CONSTRAINTS, AND CHALLENGES are things we might be tempted to resist or avoid altogether. We're on our path and doing all our inner and outer work — why is our world not expanding? It can be frustrating and discouraging to feel like you're doing all the right things, but somehow, the Universe is just not opening its arms up to you.

In these moments, it's tempting to engage in behaviors that can soothe that feeling of constriction or to lose your mind in your Ego as it tries to understand and rationalize the Universe's resistance.

But this is forgetting one vital wisdom from the natural world: all things contract before they expand; all new births are preceded by contraction and discomfort. Every time you are born anew, you squeeze through the Universe's birthing canal and emerge from your cocoon, patiently persevering and leaning into the resistance and challenges that empower you to reach higher.

Finding peace and grounding through the discomfort of the Universe's contractions is all about trust: trusting the unknown, trusting your body, trusting your Soul, trusting the Universe. Know that you are being provided with everything you need but didn't know to ask for.

As with all things, the lessons we learn on our yoga mats translate into our lives, helping us embody balance and surrender. In our practice, our physical body can often feel tight. We are asked to be aware of those sensations and try to sit with them when all we really want to do is escape, panic, or push harder to push through. However, if we can process that awareness by shifting our understanding, we embrace it as a sign that we are stretching ourselves and our limits into a new, higher life. When we surrender to that growth, we can move through the tightness.

The same goes with life.

Niyamas

IN HIS YOGA SUTRAS, the ancient sage Patanjali describes the eight limbs of yoga. They flow from the external to the internal, through the mind and the body, until we reach the eighth limb, Samadhi, translated as union or integration.

The second limb, the Niyamas, are internal observances. In particular, one of the most profound spiritual elements of yoga is Patanjali's final Niyama: the practice of Ishvara Pranidhana, or "devotion to God."

Ishvara translates as Supreme Being, God, or True Self, while Pranidhana is generally interpreted as "surrender," "devote," or "be supported by." So, while the term 'God' can be loaded, Ishvara Pranidhana is about surrendering to the Divine, Oneness, the collective consciousness, or even a yogi's personal deity.

The core of Ishvara Pranidhana is about approaching our practice as an offering we lay at the feet of the Divine, surrendering our intentions, love, and journeys to a higher power. Even our smallest actions, on or off the mat, are a devotion to something bigger than us. This simple act of dedicating ourselves and our actions to the Universe is a constant reminder of our intimate connection with the Sacred.

Surrendering to the Divine is about releasing our attempts to control the flow of energy and life; it's about releasing our attachment to our expectations. When we surrender our actions and intentions as offerings to a higher power, they become part of something bigger than us. In surrendering to the Sacred, we trust that we are always provided with what we need to help us grow, and then we offer that growth back to the Source. In this way, practicing Ishvara Pranidhana helps us cultivate a deep and trusting relationship with the Sacred that will light us up from the inside out.

Direction

UNDERSTANDING WHERE WE WANT to go, where we want to be, is a challenging process. It takes a lot of soul-searching, surrendering, and listening. It takes being receptive to the guidance of the Universe, and asking questions fearlessly, seeking clarity and direction. And figuring out where we want to go is the first step of our journey! A journey is often completely non-linear, made of stops-and-starts, loop-de-loops, and growth moments.

You see, once we have a notion of direction, a crucial question arises: *How? How do I get there? What steps do I take? What is the best way?*

This is a place where we often get stuck and overwhelmed. There might be so many ways to get where we're going or so few. Some paths require difficult choices and compromises; sometimes, steps in one direction close off other options. It's a scary moment that can last a lifetime if we let it, constantly teetering on the edge of following our path, our calling.

So, once we have a notion of direction, a crucial question arises: *Can I, and will I, commit to this direction? Through the fear and uncertainty, will I trust my gut and, surrender to the Universe, and take those steps I need to take?*

Our most powerful, most impactful offering is the commitment we offer up to the Sacred when we take the first steps along our path. It says: I trust. I trust in you; I trust in me. I trust in where I'm going. This doesn't mean that we don't expect to make mistakes, to have to re-group and re-start. It means we are willing to fail, fall, learn, and grow, knowing that each step brings us closer.

Commit to your Direction. It's the crucial first step on your journey.

Mundane Magic

SOME DAYS, IT CAN feel like we have somewhere to get to. Like there's always something to be working towards or striving for. And no doubt there's an element of truth to that: we all have better Selves to meet, dreams to manifest, and worlds to change for the best. But when we get carried away in these thought processes, we can lose sight of the most important thing: we all have lives to live.

When we're so focused on where we want to get, we forget to sit and breathe with what we've got. Life is not a race to the next goalpost, whatever that goalpost may be — even if it's a very wholesome and fulfilling goalpost!

Life is about exploring ourselves and trying to understand what we need in order for the next goalpost to come to us and giving both it and ourselves the time to do that in a sustainable and nourishing way.

To use a slightly cliched phrase, *life is a journey*. We get the most out of it when we are journey-orientated rather than destination-orientated. An imbalanced focus on productivity or achieving as a marker of success and growth is a sure road to burnout, but also to building success on external validations and factors.

Success comes from within. From our ability to live every moment for its own sake and our willingness to learn and grow from it.

Success is about taking it easy sometimes. It comes from feeling easeful and comfortable in our own skins, in our own journeys, at every stage.

Success is about patience and our strength to resist the temptation to hurry through the 'mundane' or 'daily' lives we lead. Daily life is part of the journey! Appreciate my mundane life for the solid and powerful foundations it provides you with.

Courage

I FEEL LIKE COURAGE is a very misunderstood ideal these days. The word brings up images of fearless adventurers, superheroes, and people who don't seem to need any help from anyone. It makes Courage feel like an innate character trait you either have or don't. Or it makes Courage sound like it's out of reach for the vast majority of us who don't have superpowers and know fear.

This is not helpful. I know so many people who are so courageous, day after day, but who would never consider themselves as having Courage. I've seen the small, mundane acts of Courage that make real change in people's lives. I know that my acts of Courage, which shake the foundations of my comfort zone and show me how I am capable of growth, would probably not fill the pages of an adventure book. They are the banal acts of the every day, the daily choices we make to bring ourselves forward to be better tomorrow.

And this is the true nature of Courage.

It's not the absence of fear — *how can you be courageous if you're not facing something that scares you?*

It's not a dramatic act that saves the world. It's the small actions that change your world and the world of those around you

It's not being able to handle everything alone. It's knowing when to be emotionally intelligent and vulnerable and ask for help. This vulnerability, the act of asking for help in whatever capacity, is one of the most profound acts of Courage we can perform.

Courage is found in the everyday. It's the resilience to keep going. It's the faith that we will be richer in experience and wisdom tomorrow. It's knowing that the things we fear are often the key to growth.

Visshudha

THE VISSHUDHA CHAKRA, ALSO known as the throat chakra, plays a significant role in our ability to express ourselves and communicate effectively. When this chakra is balanced, we can speak our truth with confidence and clarity. We are not afraid to express our thoughts, emotions, and creative ideas, and we are not reliant on the approval of others.

However, when the Visshudha chakra is blocked, we may experience fear and anxiety around expressing ourselves. We may feel shy, withdrawn, or even arrogant as a defense mechanism. Our inner dialogue becomes highly self-critical, and we struggle to communicate our thoughts and emotions effectively.

In our daily lives, the state of our Visshudha chakra can greatly impact our interactions and relationships. When this chakra is balanced, we can communicate openly and honestly, fostering healthy connections with others. We can express our needs, desires, and boundaries and engage in meaningful conversations that promote understanding and growth.

On the other hand, when the Visshudha chakra is imbalanced, we may find ourselves holding back our true thoughts and feelings. We may struggle to assert ourselves and may feel unheard or misunderstood. This can lead to frustration, resentment, and a lack of fulfillment in our relationships.

Recognizing the state of our Visshudha chakra is an important step in our personal growth and self-awareness. It requires us to examine our inner dialogue and identify any patterns of self-criticism or fear of judgment. By cultivating a healthy inner dialogue and practicing self-acceptance, we can begin to unblock and balance our throat chakra.

Engaging in meditation, affirmations, and throat chakra-specific yoga poses can help open and activate the Visshudha chakra. These practices can help us release fears or insecurities around expressing ourselves and allow us to speak our truth confidently and authentically.

Remember, balancing and healing the Visshudha chakra is a lifelong process. It requires patience, self-compassion, and a willingness to confront and release any limiting beliefs or fears that may hold us back. By doing so, we can cultivate a healthy and empowered relationship with our voice and communication, enhancing our overall well-being and connection with others.

Joy

JOY IS SUCH A central emotion in our lives. Too often, it is treated as childish, unproductive or unprofessional. It's not the face we want to show the world. It's not the hard-working, successful, poised face we think we should present.

But it's the face the world wants and needs to see. And it's a part of us we need to touch, awaken, and accept if we want to be whole.

Yoga is many things to many people, but for most of us, it's a path to inner and outer self-improvement. We want our bodies to be better bodies, our souls to be better souls, our minds to be better minds. We want the discipline to achieve our goals.

It can sometimes be easy to forget that Santosha, contentment or happiness, is a form of self-discipline.

One of yoga's most important lessons is that happiness is found within. It's a choice we make. We practice self-discipline every time we choose to be grateful for what we have, every time we choose to be conscious of our contentment. Every time we choose joy and bliss.

This means joy, laughter, and happiness are integral elements in our journeys of self-improvement. They're not far-flung goals nor a waste of time. They are a part of us and the journey we are taking towards our Higher Selves. Let us always remember to laugh and love, together.

Pranayama
Pause

Dirga Pranayama

"THREE-PART BREATH"

DIRGA PRANAYAMA CAN HELP to calm the mind, reduce anxiety, and improve focus and concentration. It's also a great technique to center and prepare the mind at the beginning of a yoga practice.

This technique is known for its calming effects and is often used for relaxation and stress relief. Here's how to do it:

1. Sit comfortably on a yoga mat or a chair with your feet flat on the floor and your spine erect.

2. Close your eyes and take a few deep breaths to center yourself.

3. Place one hand on your lower belly and the other on your chest.

4. Take a slow, deep breath in through your nose, allowing your belly to push against your hand. This is the first part of the breath.

5. Continue inhaling, filling your rib cage with breath, expanding it outwards against your hand. This is the second part of the breath.

6. Finally, let the breath fill the upper part of your chest, causing your chest to rise slightly. This is the third part of the breath.

7. Exhale fully, letting the chest lower, the rib cage draw inwards, and the belly draw in towards the spine.

8. Repeat this process for several minutes, focusing on the three parts of the breath.

Part Six

Alignment

Energetic alignment and physical alignment are mirror worlds of each other. When our chakras, koshas, and auric field vibrate harmoniously, our body is spacious, open, and healthy. All our organs can function optimally, and our heads and hearts exist in blissful congruence.

Asanas are a crucial tool for finetuning our physical and energetic alignment. However, alignment isn't a static reality. It is fluidity and motion. It's not found in the fixed forms we perform but in the softness and the movability of our breaths and bodies as we flow as one, connected whole. Alignment is finetuned in the moments between asanas, when we flow like rivers into an ocean, only to become rivers once more.

The focus of our yoga practice is often to create physical and spiritual alignment. There are so many theories and guides, things you should or shouldn't do, and some things you should never do. These do's and don'ts can sometimes be entirely different from studio to studio, tradition to tradition. It can be so difficult to know what to do, when, and most importantly, why.

Our teachers trust their teachers and their understanding of the human body, but beyond our physical being, deep down, we are only HUMAN.

In looking for alignment, we are looking for ease and a sense of inhabiting our greatest, most vital form. This ease and vitality create the space within us where we can achieve integration, truly connecting to our mind and body as a unified whole. And this will look different for every Body.

There's no such thing as universal, objective, correct alignment. Harmonious alignment won't look the same on every Body. Each Body is an individual reality with individual needs, shapes, and experiences, and each Body deserves an individual response.

Unity

YOGA. IN SANSKRIT, IT translates to Unity.

Unity does not mean that we are all the same, conforming to belong. Unity does not mean that belonging is exclusive to certain kinds of people.

Unity means that we are different, unique, celebrated, and connected. Unity means that we travel this road together, help lift each other up, and love each other because of all the beautiful diversity we bring to each other's lives.

Unity means yoga is for Everyone. Deepening self-compassion, compassion, awareness, and acceptance, yoga helps us connect to ourselves and each other from a place of Love.

Many of us also work hard to embody these qualities off the mat as well, bringing compassion and acceptance to our relationships and interactions with the world around us. However, in the face of persistent intolerance, hate, and ignorance, the world remains an unsafe place for many people to celebrate themselves in all their beauty and for others to connect and celebrate with them.

As yogis, the most powerful thing we can do is use our Throat Chakra, Vishuddha. It's our voice, our power of expression and manifestation, our authenticity. Vishuddha bridges the heart and the mind, integrating the wisdom of both so that loving, compassionate truth may flow freely and be expressed clearly, powerfully, and impactfully.

We celebrate the Unity embodied in yoga by raising our voices to celebrate Oneness. Yoga is for Everyone. Love is for Everyone. Life is for Everyone. But these voices must be raised all the time. These truths must flow out of us always. We need to work to embody these truths in our daily lives, on and off that mat.

Many voices raised in Unity are powerful. Together, our voices can continue the journey towards Unconditional Love.

Grounding

LIFE IS ALWAYS CHANGING all around us. Just as we think we've adapted to one set of circumstances, something challenges us differently. Whether the winds of change are blowing from our external environment or own our body and mind, resistance often leads to struggle and pain. But surrender can be terrifying.

Who knows where we'll end up? When we surrender to internal or external changes, it's like standing on the edge of a cliff. There's that feeling of vertigo as we gaze into something we neither know nor understand.

Vertigo can feel a lot like fear. But with faith in our Grounding, vertigo becomes the sign that we're extending ourselves beyond our comfort zones, accepting the uncertainties, releasing attachment to expectations, and dancing with the winds of change rather than resisting them.

Grounding is essential to our ability to bend gracefully, like trees in the wind, without losing our footing. Grounding means extending our Soul Roots deep into the Earth, trusting in our capacity and the Earth's abundance. It means trusting that we are, and always will be, supported. It means holding faith in our core values, knowing they are the foundation for all our growth.

When we are firmly rooted in the Earth and our values, we can bend, we can dance, we can flow with Life and know that we will not be destabilized — or if we are, that we can always return to ourselves.

Through Grounding poses, yoga invites us to return to our bodies and feel our Earthiness. By taking this work off the mat and into our daily lives through practices like mindfulness, spending time in nature, eating earthy foods, and focusing on our bodies and mobility, we can help grow our Grounding Roots with every breath we take.

Return Home

HOME IS A SANCTUARY that transcends physical boundaries. It is a feeling of belonging, of being understood and accepted for who you are. It is the comfort of familiar faces and the warmth of shared memories. Home is where you can let your guard down and be your authentic self, knowing you are surrounded by love and support.

Returning to Home after being away can be a bittersweet experience. The flood of emotions can be overwhelming as you are reminded of the passage of time and the changes that have occurred. There may be a sense of nostalgia mixed with excitement for the future. It is a delicate balance of cherishing the memories while embracing the present moment

In these moments, it is important to practice self-care and find solace in the familiarity of Home. Take the time to reconnect with loved ones, to share stories and laughter, and to create new memories. Allow yourself to feel the full spectrum of emotions, knowing they are a testament to the depth of your connections.

Home is not just a physical place, but a state of being. It is the essence of love, comfort, and belonging that resides within us. It is a constant reminder of who we are and where we come from. No matter where life takes us, Home will always be there, patiently waiting to welcome us back with open arms.

Full Expression

YOU MIGHT OFTEN HEAR the phrase 'Full Expression' in yoga circles. While it could be tempting to interpret 'Full Expression' as taking a pose to its most intense form, yoga is about so much more than the physicality of each asana. Yoga is about the marriage of the physical, the mental, and the spiritual, and it will look different for everybody.

Asanas are simply one of the many pathways towards yoga's central purpose, settling the mind into silence — or, as the Yoga Sutras teach us, absorbing the mind in the Infinite. In this way, 'Full Expression' embodies how our mind, consciousness, and attention become fully attuned to the grounded, physical moment, aware of each sensation that builds from our movement and breath.

When we embody 'Full Expression' in our practice, we are One with our truest, most grounded selves. We're intimately aware of how emotions and physical sensations are flowing and bubbling within us, and we accept them as part of the Infinite. We let flow, and we learn to let go.

Our practice is an essential element in our journeys of self-discovery. Learning to become aware of, experience, and surrender our emotional, mental, and physical patterns is fundamental to knowing and accepting who we truly are. And knowing and accepting our true selves is vital for true, authentic Expression.

Expression in Latin means "to press outwards." We express ourselves in words and actions, and our ability to do so authentically requires us to know and accept who we truly are, to show up, to be seen and heard. When we can harness the power of Self-Knowledge, only then can we wield the power of authentic Self-Expression.

The power of Self-Expression is the power to reveal the Soul, the power to live through Love. It's an intensely healing power that brings us closer to the Divine.

Energy

WE'RE SURROUNDED BY ENERGY; we're made of energy — we are energy. Every fiber of our being, every atom, vibrates at our own unique frequency. And the same goes for everything and everyone in the Universe!

When we talk about 'getting vibes,' we mean something instinctual and intuitive: we're literally sensing the vibrations or the energy around us, and our bodies tell us how we feel about it. The frequency at which we vibrate is like our energetic signature; it's the first thing people sense about us and how we engage with the Universe in the moment. Other people's energies can affect our own, lowering or increasing our vibrations, and we reshape the energy around us as well.

Many other things impact our energies, from physical well-being to thoughts and emotions. Some emotions — love, compassion, gratitude, happiness, joy, forgiveness — increase the frequency of our vibrations. Others, like jealousy, bitterness, shame, or blame, lower our vibrations.

Many spiritual traditions revolve around 'raising your vibrations,' or vibrating at the same frequency as the Universe, the Divine, or the Sacred — the highest frequency of Unconditional Love. This is the path to higher realms of consciousness.

Raising your vibration is really about self-awareness and self-discipline. You become aware of the emotions and thoughts you are experiencing, and you can experience the emotion fully, dive through it, and emerge in a higher vibration. It's not about 'toxic positivity,' repressing low-frequency emotions, or being constantly happy. It's about leaning into impermanence, faith, love, forgiveness, self-compassion, and gratitude and embracing the full spectrum of the human experience.

Daily practices or rituals can help give you the tools to raise and keep your vibrations level. A Gratitude Journal, daily affirmations, spending time outdoors, meditation and breathwork, a creative practice — all help keep your vibrations soaring high.

Buddhism and the Body

"To keep the body in good health is a duty... otherwise we shall not be able to keep our mind strong and clear."

"Believe it only if you have explored it in your own heart and mind and body and found it to be true. Work out your own path, through diligence."

"Nirvana is this moment seen directly. There is nowhere else than here. The only gate is now. The only doorway is your own body and mind."

Unlike many spiritualities, Buddhism embraces the body. Not simply as a vessel for the enlightened Soul but as an integral aspect of our spiritual journeys. Buddhism breaks down the duality of 'mind-vs-body' or 'spirit-vs-body,' seeing the Spirit and the Body as one and the same, equal partners, and equally important in our spiritual growth

Your body is the gateway. The Buddha awakened through bodily awareness, becoming minutely conscious of his body moment-to-moment, and he taught this until his death. The body wasn't just the gateway; it was the entire path.

You are being aware of your body and its power to help you ascend. Giving your body what it needs, from the foods you eat to the movements you perform. Steering clear of bodily addictions, expectations, and unhealthy attachments. Celebrating the unique journey towards enlightenment that your body can take you on, no matter what that looks like for you. These are the lessons of yoga, lessons born on the mat but with far-reaching teachings.

In teaching us to be closer to our physical bodies, more aware of them, and more able to be lovingly disciplined in our bodies, yoga brings us closer to our Highest Selves.

Healthy bodies are receptive to the divine. They are adaptable and flexible before the storms of life. They are like trees that root themselves deeply and grow towards the stars. Love your body with the same energy you devote to the Divine because your body will take you there.

Astavakra

THE ASANAS CENTRAL TO our yoga practice are steeped in history and meaning. The legends of the saints, scholars, and heroes who gave their names to specific poses help us to look and feel deeper into each asana, bringing our awareness more powerfully into the present moment. They teach us how we can live the present moment to its most profound potential.

The story of Astavakra is one such tale. The lessons and guidance of Astavakra's life are embodied in the physical pose that bears his name.

The name itself refers to the eight (*asta*) crooked (*vakra*) angles of Astavakra's limbs, a punishment from his father, who cursed him to be born deformed.

Despite this curse, Astavakra remained loyal and devoted to his father. When his father lost a priestly debate and was banished to the realm of Varuna, lord of death, Astavakra made the arduous, painful, and long journey to the king's court, where he challenged his father's rival.

The people of the court laughed at Astavakra, because of his bent and deformed appearance. However, when Astavakra began speaking, it became clear that they were in the presence of a learned and wise soul, despite the boy's young age.

Astavakra won the debate, securing his father's freedom. The courtiers, and the king himself, became Astavakra's disciples, repenting of their mockery and judgment.

Through piety, intelligence, and perseverance, Astavakra overcame the curse of his crooked limbs to become one of the wisest, most learned, and most respected people. The many angles of Astavakrasana evoke the crooked limbs of the curse, but the key lesson lies in understanding.

Astavakrasana looks complicated, difficult, and painful — but if you know the correct technique, it's one of the easiest arm balances, one which is primarily defined by a sense of freedom. Don't judge or perform this asana based on its appearance, but rather its true substance. Embody the faith, perseverance, and intelligence of Astavakra as you go deeper into this powerful and freeing asana.

Legacy

WHEN THINKING ABOUT OUR legacy, we tend to think of the future. What will we build? What will we leave behind? But the truth is that legacies are built in the moment. And they're not about those big projects, large-scale events, world-changing speeches, or dramatic sacrifices. Legacies are woven together day by day, word by word, action by action, as we work towards our Higher Selves and strive to grow, develop, and expand.

Legacies are hard work. They require consistency, perseverance, self-awareness, and humility. They require vision and knowing when to let that vision change and evolve. They require the understanding that everything we do is building to something, from our smallest actions to our loudest words. They require the wisdom to give ourselves the grace and space to rest and to treat ourselves the way we treat others.

Legacies are built in the little things, in the moments in between. They're built in the ways we create community and engage with those around us. They're built in the ways we face challenges, failures, and successes. They're built in the ways we communicate, in the behaviors we model, and in the choices we make.

Legacies aren't about what we leave behind. They're about how we make ourselves and the people around us feel right here, right now. They're not about what we're building but what we're building towards with every breath. Legacies are about the Now.

Most importantly, legacies are not about being perfect. How we face our mistakes, how we apologize, how we try to improve and better ourselves — these are just as important as anything else, perhaps even more so. Mistakes, challenges, and setbacks are our most teachable moments, the opportunities for us and those around us to see a different way and be willing to learn.

Through yoga, you find the mindfulness and philosophy to think about Legacy differently. And through yoga, you learn and grow, every day, to build towards something bigger than yourself. The lessons you learn on the mat are so important to living the life you want to lead, and having the impact you want to have. From your mistakes to your successes, from the way you communicate with yourself to the way you communicate with students, yoga is central to your moments, to your words, to your actions — to your Legacy.

Breathing

BREATHING COMES SO NATURALLY to us that we often forget its power. It's so much more than the automatic, reflex biological function that keeps our physical bodies alive.

Breathing connects our minds to our bodies. It's a potent tool for meditation, mindfulness, connection and focus. Our breath is a center of balance between our conscious and subconscious minds, emotional and physical reactions, and mental and physical peace.

Being aware of our breathing patterns and developing the ability to manipulate and control our breath empowers us to dialogue directly with our sympathetic (fight-or-flight) and parasympathetic (rest-and-restore) responses. This means we carry the power to design our healthy physiological reactions to the world around us. We have the tools to lower our stress and anxiety levels and ground ourselves in a balanced flow of energy.

In our yoga practice, inner and outer peace are essential: we must maintain physical and mental balance. This is why breathwork is such a central element when practicing asanas. It helps us develop our skills and use one of our most powerful and natural tools.

But breathwork doesn't just help us while we're on our mat. Breathwork instills in us a way of life. One in which we choose to be aware of our reactions and to understand how we can help our minds and bodies cope better. One in which we choose to connect to the flow of divine energy with every breath.

You don't have to be a seasoned yogi to benefit from breathwork. Anything as simple as taking five deep belly breaths while you're in the shower can engage your sympathetic and parasympathetic responses. Even developing an awareness of your breath and how it changes throughout the day can be a powerful, transformative practice.

Pranayama
Pause

Samavritti Pranayama

"Equal Breath"

THIS BREATHING TECHNIQUE IN yoga involves equalizing the length of inhalation and exhalation. It is a calming and balancing practice that helps regulate the breath and brings a sense of inner peace and harmony. Here is a step-by-step guide on how to practice samavritti pranayama:

1. Find a comfortable seated position: Sit on a yoga mat or cushion with your spine straight and your shoulders relaxed. You can sit cross-legged or on a chair, whichever is more comfortable for you.

2. Close your eyes: Gently close your eyes to help bring your focus inward and minimize distractions.

3. Relax your body: Take a few moments to relax consciously. Soften your facial muscles, release any tension in your shoulders, and let go of any tightness in your abdomen or legs.

4. Become aware of your breath: Begin by observing your natural breath without trying to change it. Notice the sensation of the breath entering and leaving your nostrils or the rise and fall of your abdomen.

5. Establish a rhythm: Start by inhaling and exhaling for a count of four. Breathe in deeply through your nose, filling your lungs completely, and then exhale fully through your nose, emptying your lungs completely. Maintain a smooth and steady flow of breath throughout the practice.

6. Equalize the breath: After a few rounds of inhaling and exhaling for a count of four, gradually increase the count to six or eight, depending on your comfort level. The goal is to have an equal duration for both inhalation and exhalation.

7. Use a breath ratio: If you find it challenging to maintain an equal count, you can use a breath ratio. For example, inhale for a count of four, hold the breath for a count of four, exhale for a count of four, and hold the breath out for a count of four. Adjust the ratio according to your capacity and gradually increase it over time.

8. Focus on the breath: As you continue practicing samavritti pranayama, bring your attention to the sensation of the breath. Feel the coolness of the inhalation and the warmth of the exhalation. Stay present with each breath, letting go of any thoughts or distractions that arise.

9. Practice for a few minutes: Start with a few minutes of practice and gradually increase the duration as you become

more comfortable. Aim for at least five to ten minutes of samavritti pranayama each day.

10. End with relaxation: After completing the practice, take a few moments to sit quietly and observe the effects of the pranayama. Notice any changes in your breath, body, and mind. Allow yourself to relax and integrate the benefits of the practice.

Part Seven

Recombobulated

IN A WORLD FILLED with chaos and constant distractions, it's easy to feel discombobulated — a state of confusion or disarray. However, yoga philosophy offers us a path to recombobulation, a term coined to describe the opposite — a state of harmony, balance, and inner peace.

Yoga teaches us to find stillness amidst the chaos to reconnect with ourselves and the present moment. It invites us to slow down, breathe deeply, and tune into the subtle sensations of our bodies and minds. By practicing yoga, we can recombobulate ourselves, finding a sense of calm and clarity even amid life's challenges.

Just as discombobulation is a state of being scattered and disconnected, recombobulation is about bringing all the pieces back together. It is about aligning our body, mind, and spirit and finding a sense of wholeness within ourselves. Through the practice of yoga, we learn to integrate our physical, mental, and emotional aspects, creating a harmonious balance.

In yoga, recombobulation begins with the breath. The breath is our anchor, our constant companion throughout our practice. Focusing on the breath brings our attention inward, quieting the mind and allowing ourselves to be fully present. As we synchronize our breath with movement, we create a flow that unites our body and mind, bringing them into harmony.

Recombobulation also involves cultivating self-awareness. Through yoga, we learn to observe our thoughts, emotions, and reactions without judgment or attachment. We become aware of the patterns and habits that may be causing discombobulation in our lives. By shining a light on these aspects, we can make conscious choices to let go of what no longer serves us and embrace what brings us joy and peace.

Yoga teaches us that recombobulation is not a destination but a continuous journey. It reminds us that life is ever-changing, and our ability to adapt and find balance is crucial. Just as we find balance in yoga poses, we can find balance in our lives by staying present, flexible, and open to the flow of life.

Remember that recombobulation is within your reach the next time you feel discombobulated. Take a moment to step onto your mat, breathe deeply, and reconnect with yourself. Embrace the practice of yoga and allow it to guide you back to a state of harmony and inner peace. Trust in the process, and know that through recombobulation, you can find balance and serenity in every aspect of your life.

Strength

maitryādiṣu balāni

Through friendliness, kindness, and compassion, strength comes. Patanjali's Yoga Sutras III.24

WHEN WE HEAR THE word Strength, we usually think first of physical strength. The word is associated with being able to perform physical feats and push physical boundaries. Most of our heroes today are physically extremely strong.

Another commonly accepted definition of Strength is emotional or mental strength, showing the world our poker face and 'keeping calm and carrying on.' It's the invulnerability that comes from boundaries or barriers that make us immune to the world and ourselves.

Both concepts of Strength feel hard. This Strength is a hard edge, something sharp. It has no give; it does not yield. It's opaque or reflective. It gives little or no insight into what truly lies inside.

But if we embrace the teachings of the Yoga Sutras, Strength is soft and yielding. Strength is flexible and generous. Strength is authentic. Strength is Love. True Strength is when the body, mind, and spirit can offer compassion and kindness when the body can support the spirit's journey.

While Strength certainly does convey some level of stability (*Sthira* in Sanskrit) in being able to withstand varying degrees of pressure, including mental, emotional, and spiritual pressure, this resilience comes from Love, not fear. It comes from feeling, not hiding from our feelings. It comes from wanting the best for ourselves and others.

Patanjali teaches us through friendliness, kindness, and compassion, strength comes (III.24). The sage's guidance for finding our strength instructs us to work through the lower instincts of fear, hate, jealousy, or greed by soothing them with good deeds and kind words (*vitarka-bādhane pratipakṣa-bhāvanam*, II.33). We may initially be surprised that making such choices gives us more energy, happiness, and strength.

Good Enough

MANY OF US LOOK to others to understand whether or not we're good enough. We hold ourselves up to the standards of those around us, seeking reassurance that we're valued and worthy of being valued.

It's easier to measure ourselves against external criteria. It means we don't have to decide what is good, what is worthy, what is valued — others decide for us, and we have to try and meet those criteria. It absolves us of the responsibility to understand our values, ourselves, and our Higher Selves.

But the truth is that only one set of standards genuinely matters to us. *Our own.* And there's only one person we should seek to be valued by. Our Selves.

Understanding this liberates us from the pressure to be good enough by other people's standards. It frees us from superficial measures of success. Intimately knowing and respecting your values empowers you to prioritize becoming the best version of yourself.

Basing our journey in love and compassion, for ourselves and for others, empowers us to be our own best friend, our own best supporter. It can be just as easy to ask too much of yourself, or be too hard on yourself, when living according to your internal standards. But knowing that you're trying to be your best self and having compassion for both the successes and the growth moments is all you need to know that you are doing enough.

We can only ever ask ourselves that we do our best. Your best is always good enough because it comes from you, and you are always good enough. There is no external standard you need to meet; there is no one else you need to measure yourself by. Simply doing your best to live authentically, in line with your values, with love and compassion, is good enough.

Humanity

"We know what we are but know not what we may be."

THERE'S A REASON SHAKESPEARE has remained such an important figure in English literature. It's not just about his craft, his perseverance, or the sheer volume of his work. It's not even about his words, in and of themselves. It's about his humanity and the humanity that fills his words like wind fills sails.

Shakespeare's works consistently resonate with deep human needs, drives, and thoughts. Even centuries later, his words and the scenes he sets out before us touch something uniquely human within all of us that makes him timeless.

Change, Transformation, and Metamorphosis are themes as familiar to Shakespeare as they are to Buddhist philosophers and yogic texts.

Shakespeare's storytelling revolves around personal transformation. The magic of his words lies in the way enemies become lovers or poor men become rich. But more than that, Shakespeare's characters were unique in the literature of his time for the depth and complexity of their inner worlds and the intensity with which they responded to events around them. Shakespeare's characters develop; they develop their understanding, their personalities, and grow in response to their worlds and impact change on the people around them. They shift through confusion to a transformed status quo.

"We know what we are but know not what we may be."

This quote from Hamlet reminds us of this. We are always going somewhere, developing and transforming into something new. Who we are now provides a foundation for our metamorphosis. Even when the present seems confusing and complicated, we transform and will come out on the other side.

His words help to ground us in the present, to be grateful for what we have, but they also help us to grow wings, reminding us to be hopeful about what lies ahead.

Sitting

IN THIS DAY AND age of busyness and almost frenetic efficiency, people spend a lot of time sitting. This is not, however, the yogic sitting that empowers us to build our resilience and develop discipline in our practice. Nor is it the powerful sitting that enables us to be with our feelings and experiences in order to release them. The sitting that we do in daily life is neither physically nor spiritually restful.

From a physical point of view, how people sit during the day impedes the body from developing a balanced and resilient posture. This makes a seated meditation asana more uncomfortable and less sustainable. Our meditation is therefore less powerful in bringing us into the moment and out of time.

Sitting at a desk, driving a car, watching TV — these forward flexion positions strain the muscles supporting our spine and freeze up our hips throughout the day. Maintaining what should be a neutral and natural upright position consequently becomes tiring and painful during our yoga practice.

To deepen our seated meditation practice and re-align our physical bodies, thereby creating open channels for spiritual alignment, our asana practice can strengthen our spines and increase the flexibility of our hips. This will make our seated meditation practice more physically sustainable and spiritually empowering.

From a more spiritual perspective, intentional sitting is a gift to ourselves.

By taking the time to sit with our feelings and acknowledge them, we realize that all they really want is to be felt to move on. When we sit without sitting and set our feelings aside to deal with later, they eventually manifest as health issues. But when we genuinely sit and receive our feelings as the earth receives the rain, they bless us with their transformative powers before flowing to the Ocean.

Vrittis

SO MUCH OF THE way we experience existence is mediated through our mental processes and thoughts. This means they are central to our journey towards "the cessation of the movements of consciousness" when the Seer rests in his own unmodified state (Sutra 1.3).

However, reaching the point where movements of the consciousness, or vrittis, cease, requires flexibility, receptivity, and openness to create something innovative, to adapt, to learn, to grow. It requires awareness of our consciousness, how it fluctuates, and how we can lean into those vrittis that strengthen us.

Patanjali describes five vrittis or mental fluctuations. Let's focus on the first three. *Pramana* is correct, or right knowledge. *Viparyaya* is incorrect knowledge, or knowledge based on misconceptions. *Vikalpa* is knowledge based on delusion or imagination, a knowledge that is divorced from reality.

It can be challenging to know when we are using vikalpa or viparyaya, when we are basing our experiences on thought processes that weaken our connection to Oneness and our Higher Self rather than strengthening it. The importance is never to let ourselves get stuck and to keep looking for perspectives and true knowledge: pramana, knowledge that is true, valid, and reliable by direct perception, inference, or authoritative testimony.

The words of French artist Francis Picabia come to mind: our heads are round so our thoughts can change direction. We are born to fluctuate, to explore, to try, to learn, to grow, until we find our splendor, our unmodified state. We can't do that by repeating the same behaviors, cycling through the same thought patterns, or relying on misconception (viparyaya) or delusion (vikalpa).

When we understand that we are headed in a wrong direction, based on viparyaya or vikalpa, we can change direction to search for pramana. We can shift our mental movements until we are in the right place to cease them.

Manifestation

THE UNIVERSE FULLY SUPPORTS what you want, but it's up to you to go for it.

We hear a lot about the power of manifestation- the universe's ability to provide and our capacity to receive. But the universe helps those who help themselves.

Manifestation doesn't mean we get to sit back and relax, waiting for success to drop into our laps. Manifestation means taking action, showing up for ourselves and our Higher Selves in meaningful ways, whether large or small.

Action is the most important part of manifesting. It can take many forms: sometimes, action looks like physical or emotional movement; sometimes, it looks like stillness. Either way, a decision is made: the decision to go for it, to DO what is right for you at this moment, whether that be quitting a job, moving to a new home, making a new friendship, or cutting off an acquaintance, or simply taking some time to retreat into yourself. Action is deciding and owning that decision.

When we decide to act for ourselves, we meet the universe halfway, entering a powerful cosmic handshake that will see our worlds evolve and change — not always in the ways we expected or wanted, but usually in the ways we need.

The universe is waiting, with hand outstretched, for us to reach up for it. The expression 'reach for the stars' isn't just about aiming high. It calls us to reach out into the cosmos, ready to grasp the cosmic hand that will guide us to unlock the next steps of our journey. It calls us to let go of fear and to go for it, to make the leap of faith, to make that decision, and to take the action that will bring us forward.

Trusting the Details

IT'S EASY TO GET caught up in the big picture and overlook the importance of the small details. We often rush through tasks, seek instant results, and neglect the process. However, yoga teaches us the significance of trusting the details and embracing the journey.

In yoga, the practice is not solely about achieving the perfect pose or mastering advanced techniques. It is about being present in each moment, paying attention to the subtle nuances of our bodies, breath, and mind. It is in these details that we find the true essence of yoga.

When we step onto our mats, we are encouraged to listen to our bodies and honor their limitations. We learn to trust the sensations and signals they provide, allowing us to adjust and modify as needed. By focusing on the details of our alignment, breath, and energy, we cultivate a deeper connection with ourselves and our practice.

Trusting the details in yoga also extends beyond the physical aspect. It involves embracing the philosophy and principles that guide our practice. Yoga teaches us to be mindful, compassionate, and non-judgmental towards ourselves and others. It encourages us to observe our thoughts, emotions, and reactions without attachment or aversion. By paying attention to these subtle details, we better understand ourselves and the world around us.

Off the mat, trusting the details can profoundly impact our daily lives. It reminds us to slow down, be present, and appreciate the beauty in the ordinary. It encourages us to approach tasks with mindfulness and intention rather than rushing through them to reach the end result. By trusting the details, we open ourselves to new possibilities, deeper connections, and greater fulfillment.

Trusting the details can be challenging. It requires patience, discipline, and a willingness to relinquish expectations. However, the rewards are immeasurable. By embracing the process and trusting the details, we cultivate a sense of inner peace, resilience, and self-awareness.

So, the next time you find yourself rushing through life, take a moment to pause and reflect. Trust the details, both in your yoga practice and in your daily life. Embrace the journey, savor the small moments, and allow yourself to be fully present. Remember, it is in the details that the true magic of life unfolds.

See

LOOKING AT THE WORLD around us, some days it seems easier to choose not to see anything at all. If we cannot see, we do not have to reflect upon, act upon, or even feel those deep issues that seem entirely out of our control and power. If we cannot see, we can choose to ignore.

But if we cannot see, we cannot create positive change. If we cannot see, we cannot face the problems that impact our lives and the lives of others. If we cannot see, we cannot deconstruct.

So, it is a choice. To live in blindness, superficially happy, with self-imposed blinkers keeping our suffering and the suffering of others out of sight. Or to live with our eyes and hearts open, aware of the ugly parts of the world and our societies, hoping to impact change where we can.

But especially if we choose to See boundaries for our own mental and emotional well-being are essential: as individuals or even as groups, we cannot possibly control, fix, or change every imperfection in this world. So, we must try to act where we are able, accepting what we can't change and changing what we can.

In the words of 20th-century social activist James Baldwin, *"Not everything that is faced can be changed, but nothing can be changed until it is faced."*

James Baldwin was a Black gay writer and activist who fought for social change, and in this quote, he recognizes that not every injustice can be made right. However, positive change will never come about unless societal weaknesses are faced. You must acknowledge a problem is present before you can even begin to try and deconstruct it.

It is also essential to know this: *you are not alone.* When we choose to See together, we choose to stand for a better world together. And together we are Strong.

Experience and Mistakes

"Experience is the name everyone gives to their mistakes." Oscar Wilde

THE FEAR OF MAKING mistakes is often what keeps us from true growth. The image and ideal of success we are presented with through social media, pop culture, and work culture is perfection. Not only does being successful require perfection, but it also feels like the road to success needs to have been perfect. So, when we make a mistake, we perceive our own failure. And the fear of failure keeps us from trying.

There are two things here that I feel very strongly about. When people talk about 'success' or their 'mistakes,' I always want to hold them and ask them: success by whose standards? Mistakes by whose standards? Whose idea of success are we measuring ourselves against?

I want to start by rethinking success because success is highly individual and personal. There's no universal measure of success. Success is what YOU need to live YOUR best life, whatever that looks like for you. And I guarantee you that no one's best life is defined by perfection.

Perfection is stagnant and still. Perfection is a shallow pond with nothing living within it, no wind playing on its surface, no leaves falling in from the trees above, and drawing beautiful ripples. Perfection has nowhere to go.

So, when we let go of the idea of perfection, we see that there are no such things as 'mistakes' because there is no right or wrong way to grow. Every so-called mistake is a lesson learned, and I know it sounds cliché — a growth opportunity. The 'mistake' itself is much less important than our attitude towards it.

When we use 'mistakes' as teachers, they become an enriching experience essential to our growth and journey. Mistakes are not mistakes. They are lessons and teachers.

Pranayama

Pause

Simhasana Pranayama

"Lion's Breath"

THIS POWERFUL BREATHING TECHNIQUE in yoga helps release tension, reduce stress, and improve focus. It involves a specific breathing pattern combined with a lion-like facial expression. Here is a step-by-step guide on how to practice Simhasana pranayama:

1. Find a comfortable seated position: Sit on a yoga mat or cushion with your spine straight and your shoulders relaxed. You can sit cross-legged or on a chair, whichever is more comfortable for you.

2. Close your eyes: Gently close your eyes to help bring your focus inward and minimize distractions.

3. Relax your body: Take a few moments to consciously relax your body. Soften your facial muscles, release any tension in your shoulders, and let go of any tightness in your abdomen or legs.

4. Take a deep breath: Inhale deeply through your nose, filling your lungs completely. Feel your abdomen expand as you breathe in.

5. Exhale forcefully: Open your mouth wide and stick out your tongue as far as possible. Exhale forcefully through your mouth, making a "ha" sound. As you exhale, contract your abdominal muscles and engage your throat muscles to create a strong and audible exhale.

6. Simultaneously, stretch your facial muscles: As you exhale, open your eyes wide, widen your eyebrows, and gaze at the space between your eyebrows (the third eye). Open your mouth wide, stretching your tongue downward and curling its tip toward your chin. Simultaneously, contract the muscles at the back of your throat, creating a roaring sound like a lion.

7. Repeat the breath and facial expression: Inhale deeply through your nose, then exhale forcefully through your mouth while stretching your facial muscles and making the roaring sound. Repeat this breath and facial expression for several rounds, maintaining a steady rhythm.

8. Focus on the sensations: As you practice Simhasana pranayama, bring your attention to the sensations in your throat, mouth, and face. Feel the release of tension and the sense of liberation as you exhale forcefully and make the roaring sound.

9. Practice for a few minutes: Start with a few minutes of practice and gradually increase the duration as you become

more comfortable. Aim for at least five to ten minutes of Simhasana pranayama each day.

10. End with relaxation: After completing the practice, take a few moments to sit quietly and observe the effects of the pranayama. Notice any changes in your breath, body, and mind. Allow yourself to relax and integrate the benefits of the practice.

Part Eight

False Identification

False identification is confusing the nature of the seer or Self with the nature of the instrument of perception. In other words, false identification happens when we mistake the mind, body, or senses for the true Self.
—Yoga Sutra II.6

PATANJALI DESCRIBES US AS Souls who have a mind and a body. The Soul is the Self, or the Seer, yet it cannot perceive on its own. It needs the mind, and it requires the body.

However, our minds and bodies are constantly subject to the fluctuations of our environments, emotions, and mental habits. They're not the most reliable perceivers! And the mind has no awareness; it can only perceive its own reality: the mind is the same as it thinks. Our Ego then works hard to convince us that the information we process through our minds is the TRUTH.

This often leads to our identifying ourselves with our Ego and our mind's reality rather than Truth. We think we are our minds and bodies, identifying ourselves with our thoughts, feelings, and personal experience — but the mind and body can only perceive from the outside.

When asked who we are, we usually answer with names, occupations, achievements, capabilities, and other external things that are likely to change. And when they do change, we feel stripped of our identity.

That's because our Ego and mind cannot honestly know us. But our Self knows the Ego. Think of it this way. Look at your thumb. You know your thumb, but your thumb does not know you. Similarly, the Self is aware of the Ego, but the Ego does not know the Self.

Since the mind and Ego are what they think, spending time in thought-free meditation brings us closer to our authentic Self. As yogi and author Dennis Hill said: *"We have spent our life identified with the contents of awareness (thoughts, feelings, and personal history); it is time to know ourselves as awareness itself."*

Slowness

WE CAN LEARN SO many pearls of wisdom from our yoga practice, both on and off the mat. There will be times for introspection, warmth, rest, and recovery. In that, the most important thing to find is Slowness. Being unhurried in our actions, our reactions, our reflections. Taking the time to grow. Accepting that growth is often slow.

Yoga teaches us that the process and journey are just as important as the destination or the result. In fact, it's an integral element in achieving that result or reaching that destination. But most importantly, it's a journey that evolves within us. It's not a journey measured in miles but in ideas, attempts, mistakes, understanding, and awareness. It's a journey measured in how well we come to know ourselves and to understand ourselves. It's a journey to develop insight.

Seeing into ourselves deeply enough to understand what we see requires practicing *Shani*. Shani is embodied in the intentional slowing down between impulse and reaction, watching, understanding, and transforming the process. It empowers us to practice mindfulness, giving us the choice of responding so we are not passively controlled by impulse.

The first steps towards Shani can be deceptively simple: observation and awareness. Watching ourselves. Noticing ourselves. But this can be difficult. We tend to perform our reactions for an external audience only; our awareness is focused on our exterior environment. Bringing that awareness to our internal processes is the first step to intentionality and mindfulness.

Take the time to rest deeply and watch yourself. Take an introspective journey, whether through yoga, journaling, or contemplation, to become aware of your internal processes. Notice how you transition from impulse to reaction. And then try to do it slower.

Self-Compassion

EVERYDAY ROUTINES AND HABITS can be thrown off course a little, making us feel like we're losing control of ourselves, our discipline, and our intentions. Whether it's our eating habits, exercise routines, work schedules, or little things we do to keep ourselves grounded, the festive season has a way of bursting into our lifestyles like an explosion of chaos.

When our habits are interrupted or changed, it's easy to slip into self-criticism, fear, and a what-the-hell attitude. The inner critic can get very loud in our ears.

Today's society encourages and even idolizes that rock-hard self-discipline and unforgiveness, perpetuating the idea that it's the only way to succeed, progress, or achieve our goals.

But yoga teaches us that self-compassion is key. Being unforgiving towards yourself is not a sign of commendable self-discipline, but that Ego is taking the reins. This Ego consciousness, or *Ahamkara*, is the sense of an individual Ego that colors our impressions of the world and of ourselves.

It fuels a sense of separation from Oneness and our Higher Selves. To stay grounded in your Higher Self and purify the mind of Ego consciousness, embrace self-compassion rather than self-criticism.

In Patanjali's Sutras, we learn about leaning into self-compassion as a path towards enlightenment. Sutra 1.33 describes compassion in the face of suffering as a practice to purify the mind and increase serenity. At the same time, Sutra 2.30 defines the first Yama as Ahimsa, or non-harming, encompassing words, thoughts, and actions. The most significant test of compassion and ahimsa is whether we can practice them towards ourselves. After all, as above, so below: the way we treat ourselves ripples outwards.

Intentions vs. Resolutions

ANY TIME THERE IS a new calendar year, there is a new beginning, a fresh page. But not wholly fresh: we build each new beginning on what we've learned the previous year. We release those patterns and aspects that no longer serve us; we integrate truths, wisdom, and intentions that help us grow. To mark this transition, many of us set resolutions. However, only about 10% of people finish the year having achieved their resolutions.

As a yogi, every time I step on my mat, it is an opportunity to reflect and create new intentions for my practice and life. I release and integrate, breathe and grow with every asana, with every meditation. My intentions are an intimate part of my daily life: sustainable and transformative. But what's the difference?

Resolutions tend to focus on things we want to change — things we are currently unsatisfied with. This means resolutions come from a place of lack and negativity. They focus on what we don't yet have or what we have not yet become. Resolutions are ego-based. They start with 'I will' and look to the future.

Intentions are soul-based. They come from a place of abundance, appreciating what we have, who we are, and what we can create from this. Rather than starting from what we want to become, intentions focus on who we want to be. They begin with 'I am' and look to the present. That means you can reflect and create intentions every day, every practice, every breath. But you can also set intentions at important transitions, like New Year, to guide your practice throughout the year ahead.

Resolution: I will lose 15 kgs.

Intention: I am healthy; my body reflects my vitality, self-love, and radiance.

Grounding in Your Higher Self

THERE ARE MANY WAYS to approach grounding. I have two main approaches to grounding that help me live in the now and fully in my body.

At the beginning of a yoga class, I might invite my students to ground down through the sit bones or the soles of their feet. It's an invitation to return to Earth from wherever our minds are taking us, be it the past (regret) or the future (worry). It's also a call to come back to our bodies. To inhabit them fully. To live in connection with our physical Self, our Annamaya kosha, so that we may build ourselves into a truer vehicle for our Atman, our eternal soul. With each asana, our connection to the Earth and our physical Self grows deeper and stronger.

But there's also an aspect to grounding directly linked to the atman. I frequently talk about being grounded in your core values, knowing the values that bring you closer to your Higher Self, and trusting in your connection to them to guide you along the journey.

While your body connects you physically to the Earth, your core values connect you spiritually, rooting you deeply and firmly in the Earth's embrace, in the core of Oneness, so you can grow tall and strong. So that you can weather any storm, flowing and dancing in the wind but never losing your spiritual feet.

When you are present with yourself and your values, you are powerful and unshakeable.

Our Journey with Others

WE OFTEN TALK ABOUT being on a journey. We're following maps and paths that resonate with us. Or we're haphazardly making our own as we go. We attune ourselves to our inner compass, becoming the only true experts on our journeys.

But journeys, while primarily internal adventures that empower inner growth, are not solo missions. We might be lone wolves as we walk our way, but we are not alone wolves. People are part of our trails. Soul guides who shine a light on the stretch of road ahead. Companions who may walk part of the way with us. Those who illuminate paths that don't resonate with our enlightenment. Those who try to hold us back show us how powerfully we need to move forward.

We rarely think of the fact that we might be helping someone draw their own map. We might be the soul guide, the companion, the warning, the barrier. Because everyone is figuring out their maps as best they can, and if we're in their lives, chances are we're on their map.

We get to choose how we appear on that map. We can be a source of inspiration and support, offering guidance and encouragement to those navigating their own journey.

By sharing our experiences and wisdom, we can help others find their paths and discover their true potential. We can be the light that illuminates their way, reminding them that they are not alone in their struggles and that they have the strength to overcome any obstacles they may encounter. Our presence in their lives can catalyze growth and transformation, empowering them to become their best version.

On the other hand, we also have the power to hinder someone's progress and ability to find their way. Our negative influence or lack of support can create barriers and obstacles that prevent others from reaching their full potential. It is important to recognize our impact on others and be mindful of the energy we bring into their lives.

By choosing to be a positive force, we can help others draw their maps with confidence and clarity, allowing them to navigate their journeys with grace and resilience. Our actions and words can shape the paths of those around us, and by choosing to be a source of love, kindness, and understanding, we can make a lasting impact on their maps.

In Between

SOMETIMES, THE MOMENTS IN between are the most challenging — after we've had friends or family over, passed the exam, or submitted the project... When we're back to life. Life in all its mundane, routine, humdrum colors.

Finding focus or motivation can be challenging. It can feel like the Sacred floated away with the last remnants of our more intense and fulfilling experiences.

In moments like these, it's important to ground ourselves in the knowledge that the line between Sacred and Mundane is of our own making. The Sacred is not reserved for sages or the most advanced yogis. It exists within all of us, and we can tap into its endless flow whenever we want.

Whether it's in your daily yoga practice, how you wash the dishes, the pleasure you take in being outdoors, or the deeper purpose that you know lies behind everything you do, the Sacred is there. It's in the attention that we bring to what we are doing. Our profound attention, our deep awareness, has the power to transform the Mundane into the Sacred.

In the words of yogi Sadhguru, nothing happens without the active involvement of the Divine, of Creation. From setting up a large project to setting the table, from feeding a gathering of family and friends to feeding only yourself — the same energy nourishes each act.

Those moments in between echo with the same Divine energy as our more outstanding experiences. Perhaps even more so, because they afford us the time and space to truly come back to ourselves and connect with the Sacred within us independent of what is happening in the world outside.

Love

LOVE IS ALL AROUND us, all the time. It is within us. It is us. Love for ourselves, Love for others, Love for the world. Unconditional, Universal, Divine Love.

In the Yoga Sutras, Patanjali puts the definitions of yoga into words. He creates the roadmap to reach an enlightened state where we rest in our true Selves and nature.

When we rest in our true nature, we rest in infinite Love.

> Yoga Sutra 1.3 tells us: *tadā draṣṭuḥ svarūpe-'vasthānam.* "At that time (the time of concentration), the seer rests in his own (unmodified) state." Our unmodified state---our true nature---is joy and, by extension, infinite Love. As translated by Nischala Joy Devi, Sutra 1.3 reads: "United in the heart, consciousness is steadied, then we abide in our true nature, joy."

It is our true nature to be happy, loved, and peaceful. To know ourselves and rest in joy. There are no conditions to meet or prerequisites to our happiness. We ARE happiness.

The expansion of this joy is infinite love, which encompasses and then transforms everything it touches. That means, when we quiet ourselves and cease the fluctuations of the mind, we are One with Infinite Love. It is our Truth to be always connected to Infinite Love.

When we recognize and embrace our true nature as beings of infinite love, we not only experience profound joy and peace within ourselves but also radiate that love outwards, touching and transforming everything and everyone around us. Our connection to infinite love is unbreakable and eternal; through this connection, we can truly make a difference in the world.

By embodying love in our thoughts, words, and actions, we become a beacon of light, inspiring others to awaken to their inherent love and create a ripple effect of love and compassion in their lives. Love is the essence of our existence, and when we live in this place of love, we can create a world filled with harmony, unity, and boundless possibilities.

Time

WE OFTEN THINK OF Time as the benevolent divinity blessing our next move. "I'm just waiting for the right Time." "It's not the right Time." But Time is a tricky lady. While she may provide us with the space to prepare ourselves or for things to align on our path, she can make us comfortable with waiting.

There's a delicate balance between having the wisdom to wait for the best circumstances and having the bravery and faith to take action. The Perfect Time doesn't exist. The Right Time exists but is a joint operation between our intentional actions and Time herself. We need to actively work with Time, not passively wait for her to line things up for us.

There's the feeling that Time brings us Opportunity by lining up the perfect circumstances for us to leap.

But Opportunity isn't a miracle visited upon us. It's a doorway that we build frame by frame, joint by joint. It's a doorway that we build over time, with Time, keeping our intentions and values in mind so they guide our hands and our partnership.

Everyone's Doors will look different. Some may be made of wood, glass, or metal. Some may have handles, and some might not. Some might even have locks. But with Time, we can also build the key.

And only we know when our Door is ready. When we let go of the idea that Time will bestow perfect conditions upon us, we can work with Time to ground and center ourselves, to know, in our bones, in our Soul, when our Door is ready, when it's the Right Time for us to walk through it.

Service

LIVING IN THE LIGHT means being of Service. It is not external, superficial service, but deep transformative service that comes from Love and Compassion — the kind of deep service that ripples out from within you and touches the world.

This doesn't mean you need to go out of your way to volunteer in far-flung places or work with at-risk youth — unless you want to and feel called to do so. Being of deep service is about HOW you do what you do, not WHAT you do. It's about doing what you are meant to do, what you are called to do, from a place of deep compassion and love.

In order to be deep, the service you share with the world needs to be something that brings you Joy and Fulfilment. You can't be of service if you resent your work and are unhappy. So, the first step to deep service is to figure out what you have to share with the World, what you want to share with the World, and how you want to share it. Base your service on your Truth, your Gifts, and your Joy. Joy creates Joy.

It doesn't necessarily need to be your full-time paid job. If you love gardening, help people with their allotments. If you love animals, put yourself out there as a dog walker or a pet sitter. Love music? Play somewhere other people can hear and enjoy it. Smile at the shop assistant. Stack your plates for the waiter. Hold the door.

Service is an action AND an attitude. Any job or activity you undertake from a place of light shines bright and elevates everyone around you, including yourself.

Pranayama
Pause

Bhastrika Pranayama

"Bellows Breath"

THIS BREATHING TECHNIQUE IN yoga helps to energize the body, increase oxygen intake, and clear the mind. It involves forceful and rapid inhalations and exhalations. Here is a step-by-step guide on how to practice Bhastrika pranayama:

1. Find a comfortable seated position: Sit on a yoga mat or cushion with your spine straight and your shoulders relaxed. You can sit cross-legged or on a chair, whichever is more comfortable for you.

2. Close your eyes: Gently close your eyes to help bring your focus inward and minimize distractions.

3. Relax your body: Take a few moments to relax your body consciously. Soften your facial muscles, release any tension in your shoulders, and let go of any tightness in your abdomen or legs.

4. Take a deep breath: Inhale deeply through your nose, filling your lungs completely. Feel your abdomen expand as you breathe in.

5. Begin the bellows breath: Exhale forcefully and rapidly through your nose, pushing the air out with a strong and quick contraction of your abdominal muscles. This exhalation should be short and powerful.

6. Inhale forcefully: Immediately after the forceful exhalation, inhale forcefully and rapidly through your nose, expanding your abdomen and filling your lungs with a quick and powerful breath.

7. Continue the rhythm: Maintain a steady and rapid rhythm of forceful inhalations and exhalations. The breath should be forceful, but not strained. Keep the movement of your abdomen and chest dynamic and rhythmic.

8. Focus on the breath: As you practice Bhastrika pranayama, bring your attention to the sensation of the breath. Feel the movement of the air in and out of your nostrils, the expansion and contraction of your abdomen and chest, and the energy flowing through your body.

9. Practice for a few rounds: Start with a few rounds of Bhastrika pranayama, gradually increasing the duration as you become more comfortable. Aim for at least five to ten rounds of Bhastrika pranayama each day.

Part Nine

You Have Power

IT'S EASY TO GET swept up in the things we can't control or impact. When we get pulled under by national or global-scale events and issues, we tend to focus on the things we can't do. We CAN'T stop things from happening, we CAN'T save everyone affected, we CAN'T change policies. We feel like we can't have Impact.

This makes us feel powerless and unmotivated. It can also be very paralyzing and anxiety-inducing. When we're convinced we can't have a positive impact on a large scale, we also tend to give up on having a positive impact on a smaller scale. It feels like nothing we do is making the world a better place.

But we need to remember that the large scale comprises a myriad of smaller scales. That the world is made of millions of small worlds, all co-existing and crossing over in unpredictable and wild ways.

There are so many things we can't control. I can't end world hunger or poverty. I can't snap my fingers and make racism go away. But I CAN control how I engage with my little world and the worlds that encounter mine.

I can help the people whose worlds meet mine feel better, feel valued, and feel human. I can leave light footprints and happy memories in the lives I touch. I can care for my family and friends so that they feel empowered to live fulfilling lives. I can advocate and vote meaningfully in my community.

When we focus on what we can do, our impact ripples outwards in ways we can't always predict.

Emotions

EMOTIONS ARE A CENTRAL and vital part of our lives and journeys. The love, happiness, and joy that punctuate our experiences and make the days feel magical and full of potential are so important. But the sadness, discomfort, or anger that make us feel powerless, uncomfortable, and out of control are equally important.

We are not our emotions. We are not sadness when we feel sad. We are not anger when we feel angry. Rather, sadness or anger rest on our hearts for a while, responding to something specific. It could be an external or internal trigger; it could be logical and rational or entirely abstract and human.

No emotions are negative, harmful, or 'worse than' other emotions. Just as happiness and love are worthy of being felt, explored, and experienced, so too are anger and sadness. There is no need to avoid them or deny them.

On the contrary, anger, sadness, and other emotions frequently perceived as 'negative' are vital signals that alert us when something is not suitable for us when something is in the way of our purpose, our calling, our values, and our best lives.

Discomfort, in particular, is a powerful teacher. Noticing our discomfort tells us so much about the types of boundaries that have developed around our hearts, and leaning into that discomfort helps us understand where they come from. When we understand them, we can improve or transform them, improve ourselves, and grow as people.

So, lean into those emotions. Sit with them. Experience them fully. They are telling you that something needs to change.

Lenses

National Geographic photographer Dewitt Jones said,

"Every day, we get to choose what lens we see the world with. It's always our choice."

That's the joy of photography. Finding the beauty in what is right in front of us. Finding the perfect lens to bring out the best in the world around us. Sometimes it takes a little time. We need to change our position, try a few lenses, and take deep breaths.

Our first impression of what is right in front of us doesn't have to be our only, or our last, impression — although, in the moment, this can be hard to remember. When things look bad for us, when we feel surrounded by chaos, darkness, and despair; when we can't find motivation or interest - we can change our lens.

With each change of lens, we can focus on something new. We can bring light to something that wasn't visible before. We can shift the lens away from those things that make us feel out of control. We can choose how we see the world around us.

Changing our lens allows us to celebrate potential and possibilities. To see where Light shines and to see where it can shine. Changing lenses brings new, previously unseen paths to light.

Empowering ourselves to transform how we see the world means empowering ourselves to choose. When our first, second, or even third impressions of the world don't bring us joy, we can choose a lens that Lights everything up.

Meditation

"Meditation is the road to enlightenment." Sogyal
Rinpoche

SOGYAL RINPOCHE IS ONE of the world's most highly regarded
Buddhist monks. His knowledge, humility, and insight
inspire me every day to show up for myself and others, and
dedicate myself to my practice on and off the mat.

His words on meditation and its core role in discovering our
true selves have resonated with me very deeply.

Through meditation, we undertake a journey to discover our
true nature. In the same breath, we discover the stability
and faith that empower us to live well and, in the words of
Sogyal Rinpoche, to die well as well. We learn to watch our
thoughts and emotions come and go and to let them flow
without reacting, responding, or feeling the need to control
and repress them.

We learn to let them arise without clinging to them or imagining that they are us. Like walking through a forest full of trees, we know to let our thoughts be and accept them in all their different forms, shapes, and sizes — without judgment, without fear, without attachment.

By taking the time to sit quietly and dive deep into our innermost nature, we perceive how our mindset and thought patterns are holding us back. When meditation becomes a core part of our practice, suddenly, it becomes far easier to create the kind of life we want.

Looking Back

LOOKING BACK GETS A bad reputation. We're flooded with messages about moving forward and forging ahead. About linear progress toward a goal. Reflecting is sometimes seen as a waste of time and energy when we could be barreling towards our future so much faster.

Looking back can also be painful. For many of us, there's a lot in our past that we would prefer not to see again. The experiences we've had, the people we once were, the people we once knew — we're more comfortable if they say hidden.

Flip the narrative on looking back. We each know, deep in our bones, that we cannot move forward meaningfully without first learning from the past. Learning from the past requires us to look back with self-awareness and intentionality.

Looking back is also an essential part of healing. Hurt, trauma, the spiritual scars we carry can only be healed with forgiveness. First and foremost, with forgiveness for ourselves, and then forgiveness for others. To choose to forgive, many of us must first choose to see. We cannot forgive what we ignore.

So, as difficult or uncomfortable as it can be, choose to look back. And choose to smile.

Surrender

LIFE CAN BE STRESSFUL and challenging. We're constantly juggling lists and expectations: what needs to be done, what should be done, what we would like to do, and what others feel and think about what we do.

At times, we encounter resistance, whether it's lack of time, lack of access or opportunity, or lack of motivation—to work, to parent, to plan, to engage...

Giving up sometimes feels like the easiest or the only option in moments like these. And it's true that we're often told to release, to surrender, to stop fighting.

But giving up and surrendering is not the same. Giving up looks like turning away. Surrendering looks like letting another perspective come into focus. And that requires us to remain present with compassion, faith, and perspective.

So, you wait. Breathe and lean into the resistance. Show up. Release expectations of what this would look like and see it for what it is. See yourself for what you are in this moment. Present and adaptable.

Make space for that new perspective that considers the resistance, holds compassion for it, and asks that you humbly arrive in the moment as you are.

Persistence

ONE OF THE PHRASES I've heard most in my life, and it's the same for many people, is: try, try again. Persistence is drilled into us as a simple, straightforward virtue.

For me, there was always something that needed to be added to this advice, which often follows a perceived failure. If you fail and try again, how will the outcome be any different the second time around? Or the third?

As I've grown into myself and deepened my relationship with myself, I've realized that there is no such thing as failure. Whenever we don't achieve something as we thought we would, it's a treasured opportunity to learn something. We don't fail; we're given a chance to see things differently to live differently.

When we see something as a failure, we don't see the opportunity to learn. And if we try again without learning, all our efforts will lead to the same result. Without insight and learning, persistence is repeating the same process, leading to the same outcome.

When people around me face challenges they struggle to overcome, I advise looking, learning, and trying again differently.

This advice aligns with a lesson from the Bhagavad Gita. In the Gita, Lord Krishna teaches the importance of self-reflection and self-awareness. He emphasizes that true growth and transformation come from understanding our nature and the world around us.

By examining our actions and their consequences, we can gain insight and make wiser choices in the future. This concept is echoed in the idea of learning from perceived failures and trying again differently. By approaching challenges with a mindset of learning and adaptation, we can break free from the cycle of repeating the same mistakes and ultimately achieve success.

Pause

IN A WORLD WHERE we are constantly expected to be on the move, on the go, jumping from plan to plan, from growth to growth, the obsession with forward momentum means we often need to catch up.

Something that gets easily lost in the rush for progress is the value of stillness. If we listen to the voices of Ego, of society, then stillness means stagnation, emptiness, nothingness. It means being passive, inactive, useless.

But we know better. Stillness means actively creating that space where growth happens. Where **true** growth happens: not the rushed growth of external progress, but the intentional, focused growth of our Highest Self.

Let's go even deeper. A student recently shared this with me: ***"Wait" requires patience. "Pause" requires presence.***

This shows us the truth that stillness is incredibly active—when we are still, we are embodying and practicing virtues: patience, presence, focus, and mindfulness. And that there are different forms of stillness.

When we wait, we tend to have an expectation: we are waiting (patiently, of course) *for* something. While not a passive activity by any means, it doesn't necessarily help us to create that internal space because we are reaching for something outside of ourselves.

When we pause, though, when we suspend our expectations and the pull of the external world on our internal landscape, we are actively creating something. When we are fully present with our core values, our priorities, Love, and the Sacred, we make that space for the Divine to flow in and elevate us. Pausing is how we can move forward in true alignment with the Universe.

Self-Reliance

THERE'S A DELICATE BALANCE between the self-reliance we need to become who we need to be and putting our independence on a pedestal — a pedestal that will eventually limit our horizons and hold us back.

Being able to rely on ourselves is the greatest gift we can give ourselves. Whether that looks like finding comfort in our own company, trusting ourselves to face challenges, internal or external, supporting ourselves to remain grounded and growth-orientated, being our own best friend in terms of compassion and healing, holding ourselves accountable to our goals - self-reliance, and self-love go hand in hand.

However, we can take this too far. By placing too much emphasis on the 'self' part of self-reliance, we can start to prioritize our independence over other beautiful things, such as connection, support, trust, and forgiveness.

If we focus instead on the 'reliance' aspect of things, self-reliance becomes just one facet of Reliance. It doesn't mean that we cut off the support others can give us or that we can give to others. It means that we recognize the gifts others have to offer and how those gifts can complement our goals and journeys.

Self-reliance means that we rely on ourselves, first and foremost, to discern who else we can rely on. The best gift of self-reliance we can give to ourselves is understanding when it's safe, and even magical, to let someone else in and when it's safer not to.

Self-reliance empowers us to rely deeply and beautifully on those who complement our journeys and let them rely on us.

Polarity

IN DAILY LIFE, AS in our yoga practice, polarity, tension, difference, and opposition appear under many guises — masculine and feminine, right and left, up and down, front and back, in and out, easy and challenging, sthira and sukha, ha and tha, yin and yang.

The misconception is that one side is better or stronger than the other. That there is only enough space in the world for one side. In reality, each in tandem, the two forces need each other to create symmetry, harmony, and unity.

Each opposing force needs the other to find balance so they can dance the dance of impermanence and flow.

In our breath, that balance is called *samavritti*. As Yogis, when we can govern our breath, we can know and direct our prana, or life force energy, which governs everything we think, feel, and do. In Samavritti Pranayama, all the opposing energies — inhalation, holding, exhalation — work together in equal measure to bring us balance and focus, to harmonize the prana flowing through our nadis. We need each element of the breath to be one with ourselves.

Yoga teaches us that when we find that balance between polar opposites, we see they are all necessary for a steady mind. By exploring the differences between these energies, we discover how we can learn to harness their power — to harness the power of what seems to be opposite so that it can unite us.

Pranayama
Pause

Sheetkari Pranayama

"Hissing Breath"

THIS IS A COOLING and calming breathing technique. It involves inhaling through clenched teeth, creating a hissing sound. Here is a step-by-step guide on how to practice Sheetkari pranayama:

1. Find a comfortable seated position: Sit on a yoga mat or cushion with your spine straight and your shoulders relaxed. You can sit cross-legged or on a chair, whichever is more comfortable for you.

2. Close your eyes: Gently close your eyes to help bring your focus inward and minimize distractions.

3. Relax your body: Take a few moments to relax your body consciously. Soften your facial muscles, release any tension in your shoulders, and let go of any tightness in your abdomen or legs.

4. Take a deep breath: Inhale deeply through your nose, filling your lungs completely. Feel your abdomen expand as you breathe in.

5. Clench your teeth: Bring your upper and lower teeth together, leaving a small gap between them. Keep your lips closed and relaxed.

6. Inhale through clenched teeth: Inhale slowly and deeply through your clenched teeth, drawing the breath in through the gap between your teeth. Feel the coolness of the breath as it enters your mouth.

7. Exhale through your nose: Close your mouth and exhale slowly and smoothly through your nose. Feel the warmth of the breath as it leaves your nostrils.

8. Repeat the breath: Continue inhaling through clenched teeth and exhaling through your nose for several rounds. Maintain a steady and relaxed rhythm.

9. Focus on the breath: As you practice Sheetkari pranayama, bring your attention to the sensation of the breath. Feel the coolness of the inhaled breath and the warmth of the exhaled breath. Notice the sound of the hissing breath and the calming effect it has on your mind and body.

10. Practice for a few minutes: Start with a few minutes of practice and gradually increase the duration as you become more comfortable. Aim for at least five to ten minutes of Sheetkari pranayama each day.

Part Ten

Observing The Observer

IN LIFE, IT CAN feel like we're often dedicating a lot of energy to performing for the benefit of others. At work, we might be dedicating our performance to our bosses; in our relationships, we dedicate it to our friends or significant others. When we put clothes on, we think of how others perceive us.

A lot of our energy is wasted this way, shed here and there as we give away our power to others. If we want to walk honestly and in truth, stepping authentically into our power, we must dedicate our energy to performing for ourselves first and foremost.

With compassion and honesty, ours is the gaze that matters most. Are our actions in alignment with our core drivers, our core values? If not, why? How can we bring ourselves back to our center?

When we bare ourselves before our own gaze, we step into the role of the Observer and the Observed. We transform from being at the mercy of the gaze of others to being in the perfect balance of observing and impacting what we observe.

Yoga is the perfect example of this. As we flow through asanas, we perform much more than physical exercise — we are seeking the integration of body, mind, and breath. This requires us to be powerfully and mindfully aware of everything that is going on inside us, on a physical level, an emotional level, and a spiritual level. Only when we see everything can we bring everything together.

If we perform yoga for the gaze of others, we are not doing yoga at all. We are just doing exercise. Similarly, if we are living for the gaze of others, we are not living at all. We are just existing.

Space

WE SOMETIMES THINK OF Space as a fixed quality: our space, your space, enough space, too little space, too much space. We know we need some, we know we like to share some, and we know some people need more or less than others.

It's easy to get the impression that the amount and quality of Space we need, want to occupy, or want to share is fixed. It is as if we can predict how Space works for us and those around us, as though it were a consistent character trait.

But when we start paying attention to ourselves, to the *vritti*, or fluctuations of the mind, that sway our mental processes, it's clear our minds fluctuate differently in response to different environments and situations. Different quantities and qualities of Space are needed to help us balance ourselves out.

It's not true, for example, that introverts always need to be alone or enjoy being isolated. Nor is it true that extroverts always want to share their space with plenty of people. Space and our relationship with it fluctuate along a spectrum, just like our energies and bodies.

Understanding the quality and quantity of Space that we are craving at any given time can help prevent or cope with challenges like burnout, anxiety, and depression — *vrittis* that can be exacerbated by isolation or socialization, might be soothed by giving ourselves the right kind of Space.

Holding Space for others is also an act of service that is tailored and unique: the way we hold Space is not the same for everyone; what we fill that Space with is not the same for everyone.

Space is what we make of it.

Impact

MANY OF US STRIVE to have impact, make a difference, and bring something beautiful into the world that others will benefit from. And this is a beautiful thing.

But it can often be accompanied by feelings of powerlessness or inadequacy, with imposter syndrome rearing its ugly head. That's the voice of the Ego. In seeking to protect us, as it did when we were young and vulnerable, the Ego wants to hold us back, to keep us small, to stop us from being seen. Our impact is its greatest fear.

That's what can stop us from seeing that we each have a unique set of gifts, born of nature or experience, often both. The Soul sees these. The Soul knows that we are able and worthy to have an impact. We just have to trust it.

No matter our circumstances, we are empowered to create an Impact when we harness our unique abilities. But while we let the Ego drive, this can never truly happen.

The first step towards impact is a step inward. To descend past the layers of Ego, the loud fear, and louder powerlessness. To reach a place of such silence that we can hear the Soul whisper.

Meditation is a powerful tool for reaching this place. It quiets the voice of Ego and makes space for the Soul to speak. And the Soul can tell us how we can best Serve.

Because that's the truth of Impact, it is achieved when we understand how we can best use our gifts to Serve the Universe. So let your Soul whisper to you what your Gifts are, and you'll know how you can be of Divine Service.

Guilt and Shame

FEW EMOTIONS CAN BE as paralyzing as Guilt and Shame. They often come together, simmering to the surface from the depths of our Fear. They sit in the pit of our stomach, on our chest.

When we experience things like Guilt or Shame, it means we're dealing with an underlying anxiety. It might be a fear of rejection or judgment. Of not being or doing enough. Whatever it is, Guilt and Shame are a sign from your Ego that it is afraid of something deep down.

When we let that fear bog us down, we let ourselves get trapped into inaction. It's challenging to make brave decisions when our Ego is working hard to hold us back. Our Ego thinks it knows best, and it shouts the loudest when scared.

When faced with a wall of Fear, the best way to soothe our Ego is with *Dainya* or Humility.

Yoga teaches us that how we behaved in the past is less important than our will to grow in the present. When we respond to Ego-based emotions with *Dainya*, we remain receptive to knowledge, grace, and love, and constantly see the growth opportunities that are presented to us.

Most importantly, *Dainya* is one of the many lessons of yoga that help us release attachment to Ego and, therefore, release Ego-based emotions such as Fear, Guilt, and Shame. *Dainya* allows us to soar with our Highest Selves.

The Middle Path

YOGA IS THE JOURNEY to unity through balance: finding peace within ourselves and between ourselves and the world around us. One of the ways we can work towards this is by calming the fluctuations of the mind, not letting our streams of consciousness, our *vrittis*, get tugged and pulled this way and that way.

How? By walking the Middle Path.

> *"Yoga is not for him who eats too much nor for him who eats too little. It is not for him who sleeps too much nor for him who sleeps too little. For him who is temperate in his food and recreation, temperate in his exertion at work, temperate in sleep and waking, yoga puts an end to all sorrows." (Bhagavad Gita 6:16-17)*

The Middle Path means avoiding extremes of thought or behavior. The Bhagavad Gita tells us that the key to happiness is knowing the middle ground, flowing steadily along our path, and not letting the world around us pull us away from our journey. Never too much, never too little, always what is right for us. This means we must first know ourselves.

In practice, walking the Middle Path means keeping space for that silence and stillness where we can listen to ourselves so that we can walk the path that is right for us rather than the path pushed by society.

It means noticing the extremes around us and observing them without judgment, without taking them into ourselves.

It means always being centered in our truth and connection with the Universe.

Points of Diversion

WE ARE ALWAYS EXACTLY where we need to be to learn exactly what we need to know — although sometimes, that's more difficult to remember than others.

Sometimes, the big challenges are easier to face and easier to get motivated for. It's when we forget why we're here, in our current daily lives, doing our current daily thing, that the motivation to see how we can grow is more complicated to come by.

And sometimes, the last thing we want to do is look at how we got here.

But when we feel stuck, like nothing is quite what we expected, and we're not feeling like we thought we'd be feeling or living the life we thought we'd be living, it's essential to look back.

It's important to remember why we thought we'd be living that particular life and feeling that particular way to begin with. It's important to look at the choices that led us to this exact point to understand where our path diverged from our intentions.

Those points of diversion are NOT failures. They are lessons. They are windows into how we can be different next time. They are the bricks that solidify the foundations of our future selves. Those points of diversion are where we understand ourselves.

Just like we breathe into the discomfort that certain asanas can bring so that we can flow and grow better, so too should we breathe into the discomfort of 'stuckness,' so that we can flow and grow from it. When we stop seeing feeling 'stuck' as a failure and start to see it as the wake-up call that it is, it becomes an opportunity for us to learn to fly.

Brahmaviharas

THE DIVINE RESIDES IN all of us — we are all abodes of the Divine. Sometimes it shines through, and sometimes it's harder for us to connect with.

The Brahmaviharas are the four emotional states, Buddhist virtues, and meditation practices, which can help to bring us within the Divine — they empower us to abide within the Divine in us and consequently to be in Oneness.

A *vihara* means a dwelling place in Pali, the language in which the oldest Buddhist scriptures are written, while Brahma is the word associated with all aspects of divinity. The Brahmaviharas literally mean the divine abodes within us, the places in us where the Divine lives and where we can choose to live when we cultivate them.

The Divine lives in *metta*, loving-kindness, *karuna*, compassion, *mudita*, appreciative joy, and *upekkha*, equanimity. I like to think of them as the four faces of the god Brahma, the four paths which form the road to Ascension.

In their simplest, most superficial forms, the Brahmaviharas are the faces of our daily experiences, as we feel goodwill towards others, caring and sympathy for them, as we take joy in their joy, and as we remain self-differentiated enough so that their mental fluctuations do not affect ours.

But at their deepest, most transformative level, the Brahmaviharas are the faces of the Love that guides our intentions and actions. They are a choice that we make in the face of challenges.

Our yoga practice gives us the tools to develop each of the Brahmaviharas, and guided meditations bring us closer to each of the Divine dwelling places within us. Through yoga and meditation, we can discover and develop our capacity to Love.

Choices

WHERE WE ARE NOW is thanks to every single choice we've ever made — whether it was choosing a path or action or choosing how we responded to circumstances beyond our control.

In this way, our choices impact our future, and our present choices can tell us a lot about who we are now, how we make those choices, and what drives us.

But it is never our past choices that define who we are now. We are constantly remaking our choices and responses, continually growing from past decisions.

This is especially true for those choices that might feel, with hindsight, to have been 'poor' choices, 'bad' choices, the choices that we struggle to look in the eye. We struggle to look at them because we are judging them; we are judging the version of us that made them, and we are judging ourselves now.

To recognize those 'poor' choices, and most importantly, to truly learn from them, it's compassion that we need in our gaze, understanding for who we were then, and for the circumstances or limitations that might have led to those choices — limitations that we have hopefully acknowledged and worked on with discipline and self-love so that they no longer impact our decision-making.

When we can forgive ourselves for those choices and learn the lessons they offer us, we can move forward with more faith in ourselves and more wisdom in our hearts.

Because making choices is rarely about looking forward, it's about looking inward. When we make choices, we need to make the space and time to find the stillness in which the compass needle of our Soul can gravitate toward the choice that reflects our core values.

Faith

Judith Lasater, author of *Living Your Yoga*, writes, "Faith is a recipe made of part trust in ourselves, past experiences of life working out, and part intuitive connection with the divine."

HER INTERPRETATION OF FAITH, which has become very entangled with religion and relationships, sits well with me. True faith goes beyond faith in an external divinity or being faithful to an external person or concept. True faith is just as grounded within ourselves as in others and the Divine.

In this way, faith is a beautiful and straightforward amalgamation of yogic principles. It's a vital part of yoga, of yoga as Unity. Without faith, we cannot be truly one with ourselves and one with the Universe.

When faith starts within, with faith in ourselves, it's linked with releasing attachment, releasing expectations, and embracing a willingness to experience reality as it is. We trust that we have what we need to make the most of what the Universe offers. We allow other people and external events to unfold without asking anything of them, without judging them, without projecting onto them our fears, needs, and desires. Our centeredness, our groundedness, our connection to the Divine is a flame that shines within us and needs no kindling other than who we are. We are One with ourselves.

As Judith says, there is also an external element to faith: the Divine. We can only truly have faith in the Divine when we have released the attachments and expectations that tie us to the material world and made space for it. Only then can we see that it already shines within us and that we shine within and with the Universe.

Overwhelmed

FEELING OVERWHELMED IS OFTEN associated with negative things, like stress, obligations, or challenges. It can seem illogical or ungrateful when we feel overwhelmed by positive things, but it's normal. 'Good' things can also become overwhelming and depleting if we let them.

An added challenge when we are overwhelmed by positive things is that we often feel guilty or inadequate: I should be enjoying this; this is an amazing opportunity; I'm so blessed to have this many people I cherish who also care about me; I can do so many things that are fulfilling and bring me joy, so I should do them.

That sense of obligation, guilt, and shame, when we find ourselves swamped by 'good' things, can be very disempowering, like our feelings aren't valid or reliable, and we're 'failing' at making the most of what life brings us, 'failing' at being grateful.

It's important to realize that 'good' things can also be overwhelming, and that's okay. They require outlays of energy and time, and while they can be replenishing when we're well-balanced, if we let that balance fall into 'too much,' even good things can be draining.

Good things are only good when they are balanced with our other needs. We must not be scared to let some good things go when they cease to be good for us. For that, we need to trust ourselves.

When your body is telling you that things are too much, it's time to go back to the basics — YOU.

Your yoga practice is there to re-center yourself in self-compassion and mindfulness so that you can be fully present in the moment and in tune with your soul's needs.

Pranayama
Pause

Surya Bhedana Pranayama

"SUN PIERCING BREATH" OR "RIGHT NOSTRIL BREATHING"

THIS BREATHING TECHNIQUE INVOLVES inhaling through the right nostril and exhaling through the left nostril. It is believed to activate the solar energy in the body, increase alertness, and stimulate the sympathetic nervous system. Here is a step-by-step guide on how to practice Surya Bhedana pranayama:

1. Find a comfortable seated position: Sit on a yoga mat or cushion with your spine straight and your shoulders relaxed. You can sit cross-legged or on a chair, whichever is more comfortable for you.

2. Close your eyes: Gently close your eyes to help bring your focus inward and minimize distractions.

3. Relax your body: Take a few moments to relax your body consciously. Soften your facial muscles, release any

tension in your shoulders, and let go of any tightness in your abdomen or legs.

4. Take a deep breath: Inhale deeply through both nostrils, filling your lungs. Feel your abdomen expand as you breathe in.

5. Use your right hand: Curl the index and middle fingers of your right hand toward your palm. Keep your ring finger, pinky finger, and thumb extended.

6. Close your left nostril: Use your right ring finger to close your left nostril gently, blocking the airflow.

7. Inhale through your right nostril: With your left nostril closed, inhale slowly and deeply through your right nostril. Feel the breath entering your body and filling your lungs.

8. Close your right nostril: Use your right thumb to close your right nostril gently, blocking the airflow.

9. Exhale through your left nostril: With your right nostril closed, release your ring finger and exhale slowly and smoothly through your left nostril. Feel the breath leaving your body.

10. Repeat the breath: Continue alternating between inhaling through the right nostril and exhaling through the left nostril. Inhale through the right nostril, close the right nostril, exhale through the left nostril, and then switch sides.

11. Focus on the breath: As you practice Surya Bhedana pranayama, bring your attention to the sensation of the

breath. Notice the flow of air through each nostril and the subtle energy shifts in your body. Feel the awakening and energizing effect of the right nostril breath.

Part Eleven

Tension

TENSION IS SOMETHING WE'RE often invited to see in a negative light, something to let go of because of its impact on our minds and bodies.

Flip the script a bit here. Before focusing on releasing tension, look at the nature of tension and think about what we gain when we release it.

At its core, tension is a teacher- a visceral reaction our minds and bodies have to particular stimuli. It shows us the truth of how things are impacting us, and I think it's important to sit with that tension for a bit so it can tell us everything it's trying to communicate.

Listening to our tension means examining where we are attached, what we haven't acknowledged, and where our egos are still sensitive. Only when we truly see and acknowledge can we truly release.

When we take the time and space to examine our tension enough to release it fully, rather than calm our nervous system to get through it in the now, we gain something: insight and perception. This self-knowledge enables us to overcome these visceral reactions and let go of the attachments and fears that drive them.

So, tension teaches us to look. On the mat, it can show us where our physical resistance to certain asanas, flows, or meditations is based so we can nurture that location, giving it what it needs in order to release. Off the mat, it brings into focus the stimuli that activate an ego response, a fear response, or an anger response, showing us where we can focus on self-improvement journeys next.

We just need to learn to listen.

Clarity

"When you just sit in silence, and the wind blows through you, and the sun shines in you, and you realize you are not your body; you are everything." Anita Krizzan

CLARITY IS OFTEN THOUGHT of as a mental exercise. Getting clear on our goals, on our needs, on our boundaries, on our priorities. But getting clear on things is about so much more than mental focus.

Clarity comes from understanding the wholeness of ourselves — from our minds, to our bodies, to our souls — and then understanding that we are part of an even larger wholeness.

I like to think of clarity in its literal sense as well: when we are truly connected, we are so clear that the wind, the sun, and the Universe shine right through us because they are an inextricable part of us and we are an inextricable part of the Whole. You can literally see through yourself into the Universe, and you can see through the Universe into yourself.

That's why clarity requires that we connect the mind to the body, the body to the Soul, and the Soul to Unity. That we become One.

Yoga is the practice of returning to the Unity of body, mind, and *atman*, the spiritual essence at the deepest level of existence.

Yoga reveals the path towards Wholeness, but the most important thing to realize is that this path must be chosen both on and off the mat. In the day-to-day choices that we make, in the thousands of little things that we do every day.

Yoga, and therefore the path towards Wholeness, comprises the myriad of small choices that help us become Clear.

Ahimsa

THE YAMAS ARE THE foundations of Yoga. All progress starts with them, and the first Yama is often seen as the most important---the foundation's roots, the core of our grounding force.

For me, *ahimsa*, from *himsa*, 'hurt,' with the prefix *a*, 'not,' is the purest and most spontaneous expression of the truest, highest love. It's often translated to non-violence or non-harming; its source lies in an unconditional approving gaze on everything.

It would be easy to reduce *ahimsa* to the absence of physical violence or refraining from causing injury to others, but this would mean closing our eyes to the true complexity and depth of this beautiful Yama.

The more direct translation from Sanskrit would be 'absence of injury.' This encapsulates the absence of physical injury and mental and emotional injury; it doesn't only refer to other people but to all things in the world and, importantly, to ourselves.

When we seek to refrain from harming ourselves and the world around us, we must naturally start with our core. As within, so without: we cannot truly bring pure love to the world if we carry self-loathing self-criticism and look at the world with bitterness or envy. Outer peace starts with inner peace.

When we can gaze into ourselves with unconditional love, we can bring and project that out into the world, gazing at all things with light and compassion. From this light and compassion, we can develop the practices and habits that will help us live with *ahimsa* no matter what life throws at us.

Asteya

YOGA MEANS UNITY, WHOLENESS, Connection. Throughout our yoga journeys, we're working towards the knowledge and understanding that we are Whole unto ourselves and Whole in our Connection to the Divine.

The third Yama, Asteya, goes straight to the core of this quest for wholeness. Asteya translates as non-stealing, and, like all the Yamas, it might seem quite simple on a surface level: don't mug people in the street, don't take what belongs to someone else...most of us already embrace Asteya, right?

But, again like all the yamas, Asteya means so much more. Its significance stretches beyond the physical, encompassing intangible resources like time, peace, emotions, space. And it's about more than not taking what belongs to someone else. It means not taking what is not ours, whether it belongs to anyone else or not, and not taking what we do not need.

In this way, Asteya is connected to such notions as lack, greed, materialism, respect, abundance, and gratitude. The desire for something that we do not have, that feeling of coveting resources that we feel we are lacking, often stems from the fear that we are not enough: that we are not good enough, that we don't have enough, that we don't do enough. That we are not Whole.

Here, the principles of Asteya remind us not to desire or covet what is external to us because in our connection with the Divine, we are Whole, and we are All. We either have or can create all that we need at the moment.

Practices centered around abundance and gratitude are very helpful grounding rituals when we feel ourselves straying from Asteya, as they bring us back to the faith that we have all that we need.

Satya

THE YAMAS FORM THE moral groundwork from which the seven other limbs can grow. As such, they are the core that we can return to when we feel ourselves fluctuating or spiraling — they provide a powerful grounding force.

> "To one established in truthfulness, actions, and their results become subservient."

Satya is the second Yama. 'Sat' can be translated to 'true essence' or 'true nature,' 'truthfulness' or 'non-falsehood.' It means so much more than simply not telling lies. It means both being true and seeing true.

Seeing true is the first step to real truthfulness. How can we be true if we cannot see the truth in us or in the world around us? In this way, Satya is about understanding that there is a truth beyond our thoughts, emotions, and reactions, beyond our ego — a truth that is a glimpse into the Atman (soul). It means searching for that truth, so we are always connected to it. And it means acting with integrity and authenticity, reflecting our atman.

Importantly, this requires us to see things as they are, not as we wish them to be, nor as we have been conditioned to see them - including ourselves. It means letting go of self-delusion and expectations and being open to Seeing.

When we can do this, our actions and their results will reflect that Truth, our atman, and serve us in our journey towards the Divine.

Aparigraha

I<small>T OFTEN FEELS LIKE</small> life gives us a lot of lemons, so it can be tempting to grab as much as possible when life gives us something sweet. It's easy to fall into the trap of trying to hoard, cling onto, or control the moments of ease and abundance. But that's the surest way to struggle against ease, increase our anxiety, and show the universe that we aren't ready to handle abundance.

Aparigraha is often translated as 'non-greed', 'non-possessiveness', and 'non-attachment'. We can break it down into *'graha,'* meaning to take, seize, or grab; *'pari,'* which means 'on all sides;' and the prefix *'a,'* negates the word itself.

This Yama is about learning not to require or take more than is necessary, to keep what serves us in the now, and to understand when it is time to let go. It reminds us not to take advantage of people and situations or to let greed dictate our actions.

It's linked with the poverty mindset that too many of us are stuck in, especially in this consumerist society that always pushes us to associate success with more belongings and capital. Where society would have us believe that we never have enough, Aparigraha calls us to remember that we always have what we need to manifest what is necessary for us to grow.

Aparigraha teaches us to look within for abundance and ease, to have faith in our connection to the Divine, and ground ourselves in the Sacred within ourselves.

Brahmacharya

THIS YAMA IS USUALLY the most misunderstood. I often see it translated as 'celibacy' or 'chastity,' or associated with deprivation and sacrifice. This can make it seem removed from contemporary spiritualities or perspectives and feel like an unachievable ethical goal.

Brahmacharya comes from *Brahman*, the Creator or Higher Power, true Divinity, and *charya*, a path or way. It can be thought of as the path to the Divine, and Brahmacharya refers to behavior that keeps us on this path. The concepts of celibacy or deprivation are more linked to restraint, conservation, and prioritization.

Brahmacharya is also translated as 'the right use of energy.' Behavior is the result of how we choose to direct our energy, and Brahmacharya is, therefore about using or channeling our energy in the way that keeps us on the path to the divine: conserving our energy for this path, restraining ourselves from leaking or wasting this energy in other pursuits, and prioritizing where we channel our energy.

For many, this interpretation of Brahmacharya invites us to move away from external pleasures and happiness, build up those energies that fuel us from within, and find everything that links us to the Divine. We are the path.

To become our own path, we must learn to listen to ourselves. To our true voices, our bodies, and our Souls. To find the Silence where our Higher Selves can whisper the Divine into our hearts.

Meditation and a mindful yoga practice are the perfect tools to create that Space, to understand our energy, to see how we're using it and where we could be channeling it.

Conflict

CONFLICT AND CONFRONTATION CAN be extremely draining. Every day, we encounter people and situations that clash with our values, boundaries, and goals or how we choose to exist in the world.

However, no conflict is as draining as conflict within ourselves, and the conflict that I notice people struggling with the most is the one between their outer and inner postures.

Too often, our outer posture — how we physically inhabit the world — is not aligned with our inner posture. Our external behavior doesn't authentically project how we want to be. When that happens, the conflict that arises can deplete us of motivation and self-belief.

The first and most important step when that inner conflict arises is awareness, listening to our Souls so we know when we fall out of step with ourselves. And then, we need to ask ourselves why.

Where did the disconnect between our inner and outer postures come from? Often, it comes from a place of Ego-based fear: fear of rejection, fear of shame and guilt, fear of being different, fear of being ourselves.

When we listen to that Ego-based fear, when we let it shout louder than our Soul sings, we lose touch with Connection and Authenticity, when we fall out of Oneness.

To return to ourselves so that our inner and outer postures are united in Authenticity and Connection, we need to make the space and time to go deep.

Get to know your inner landscape again, your values and boundaries, what drives you. Get to know yourself again so you can represent yourself truthfully.

Enough

OUR MODERN SOCIETY IS very focused on action and results. Things always need to be happening, and they need to be happening NOW. We're constantly stimulated by our phones, instant communications, and what we need to do.

There's this sense that more is best — having more going on, doing more, experiencing more. But less can actually be a lot better.

'More' can become a consumer of space. It takes up physical space, mental space, and emotional space until, eventually, something (usually our well-being) has to give. It can be inauthentic and cruel.

'Less' is a creator of space. It makes room for us, for our loved ones, and for connection with the Universe. It removes the illusion of productivity and purpose from keeping busy. It can be honest and compassionate.

Less is not unproductive or wasteful. Less is fertile ground. Less is hibernation and rebirth. Less is Winter's rest so that Spring can come back stronger.

And there's something that we don't talk about very much: Enough.

Enough gives us the space to do less, and the space to be fulfilled and ambitious and forward-driven, the space to seek out More if we are guided to do so — because More that is Soul-driven and balanced out with Less can be as nourishing as Sunlight.

Taking the time to pause and replenish is vital to living a fulfilled, active, and sustainable life. If we don't retreat and hibernate from time to time, how can we hope to remain productive and creative? The Soul needs Darkness just as it needs Light, and it needs Less just as it needs More.

Dropping the Veil

WHO ARE YOU? SOMETIMES the answer feels clear, at the core of your being, from the tip of your toes to the crown of your head.

Other times, it's hazy, like there are layers of veils between your awareness and your truth. This haziness is part and parcel of the human experience: those veils are made up of our self-projection, our social roles, our jobs, our friendships, our belongings, our status — or lack thereof — which we can grow to mistake for our True Self. The True Self becomes obscured, and one of the goals of yoga is to help lift those veils and rediscover who we are.

Sutra II.6, *Drgdarsana saktyoh ekatmata iva asmita*, warns us of this haziness, or false-identification.

> "False identification is confusing the nature of the seer or Self with the nature of the instrument of perception. In other words, false identification

happens when we mistake the mind, body, or senses for the true Self."

As our yoga practice and the rituals we carry with us in our daily lives help to shed the layers of illusion and misidentification, a beautiful truth becomes self-evident: our True Self is not a single entity; it is not one truth, and we are not isolated beings — our True Self is the part of us that is connected to everyone and everything in the Universe. It is the Divine in us and in all things and will always be the core of who we are.

Pranayama
Pause

Chandra Bhedana Pranayama

"MOON PIERCING BREATH" OR "LEFT NOSTRIL BREATHING"

THIS BREATHING TECHNIQUE IN yoga involves inhaling through the left nostril and exhaling through the right nostril. It is believed to activate the lunar energy in the body, promote relaxation, and stimulate the parasympathetic nervous system. Here is a step-by-step guide on how to practice Chandra Bhedana pranayama:

1. Find a comfortable seated position: Sit on a yoga mat or cushion with your spine straight and your shoulders relaxed. You can sit cross-legged or on a chair, whichever is more comfortable for you.

2. Close your eyes: Gently close your eyes to help bring your focus inward and minimize distractions.

3. Relax your body: Take a few moments to relax consciously. Soften your facial muscles, release any tension in your

shoulders, and let go of any tightness in your abdomen or legs.

4. Take a deep breath: Inhale deeply through both nostrils, filling your lungs completely. Feel your abdomen expand as you breathe in.

5. Use your right hand: Curl the index and middle fingers of your right hand toward your palm. Keep your ring finger, pinky finger, and thumb extended.

6. Close your right nostril: Use your right thumb to close your right nostril gently, blocking the airflow.

7. Inhale through your left nostril: With your right nostril closed, inhale slowly and deeply through your left nostril. Feel the breath entering your body and filling your lungs.

8. Close your left nostril: Release your right nostril and use your right ring finger or pinky finger to close your left nostril gently, blocking the airflow.

9. Exhale through your right nostril: With your left nostril closed, exhale slowly and smoothly through your right nostril. Feel the breath leaving your body.

10. Repeat the breath: Continue alternating between inhaling through the left nostril and exhaling through the right nostril. Inhale through the left nostril, close the left nostril, exhale through the right nostril, and then switch sides.

11. Focus on the breath: As you practice Chandra Bhedana pranayama, bring your attention to the sensation of the breath. Notice the flow of air through each nostril and the subtle energy shifts in your body. Feel the calming and cooling effect of the left nostril breath.

Part Twelve

Motivation

SOME DAYS, MOTIVATION AND enthusiasm are in the air we breathe, and every inhale fills us with optimism. Other days...not so much. It can be a lack of energy, vision, drive or — whatever it is, the energy that keeps us going feels like it's missing.

In these times, we easily forget that this energy isn't an external gift. It's internal. It comes from our core, from our Soul, from our Connection. We generate that energy endlessly. It's our very own renewable resource.

Some days we have to dig a little deeper and work a little harder to get that energy moving again. Because that's what happens to us on those days when we can't pick ourselves up: our energy is stagnant, stuck, blocked, and blocking us from being our best selves.

The most important thing to remember is feeling that disconnect and despondency is okay. It happens to everyone, and it's a sign that we need to give ourselves time to reconnect.

Yoga is there for us to rekindle that Union, that Connection with ourselves and the Sacred. Your practice is your kindling, an ever-present source that nourishes your core and your Soul. Your practice is your greatest tool.

On the mat, focus on awakening the fire from within your sacral chakra, grounding it into the Earth, and flowing it up to your crown so it can cleanse and renew you from the inside. From a deep pranayama practice to a flow focused on strength and alignment, there are many ways to reconnect with your inner fire in ways that suit your body and your needs.

Be kind to yourself and trust yourself.

Duality

THERE IS THIS IDEA that we can be either soft or hard. That we can be fighters or dancers, a rock or a flower. But that we cannot be both.

We cannot reach balance if we hold on to this mutually exclusive opposition. And we would be holding on to a very superficial illusion.

The dancer might seem soft and fluid, but their body is all muscle and tone: it takes so much power to be graceful, flexible, and controlled. The flower might seem delicate and gentle, but it takes so much strength to grow out of the ground and survive the wind and the rain.

Similarly, the fighter might seem hard and strong, but they need to be fluid, balanced, and flexible to adapt to their circumstances. The rock, which appears unyielding, lets itself be carved into beautiful shapes by the wind and the water.

It is the same with our yoga practice. Sometimes, we need to focus on flow and grace, other times on strength and stability, but most of the time, we try to embody both. We need both to harmonize the mind, body, and soul to move in holistic ways.

Off the mat, when we engage with the world and the people in it, our strength is our grace, and our grace is our strength. We can make room for others without losing ourselves. We can elevate the world while remaining grounded.

True Gratitude

GRATITUDE FOR THE NICE things — family, food, your job — is easy, and let's be honest, a little cliche. Practicing this kind of gratitude is one of the steps towards happiness, but reaching that elevated level of peace requires more than the slightly fluffy and smug feeling superficial gratitude gives you.

Real peace is achieved through real Gratitude, and real Gratitude can be confronting, dark, challenging, and bring up plenty of emotions and blockages we might prefer to ignore.

Real Gratitude is being grateful for the obstacles, the challenges, the setbacks, and the bits of our lives that, on the surface, seem downright ugly.

Practicing real Gratitude forces us to actively find the light in the darkness that sometimes surrounds us. It takes work. It only sometimes comes naturally. It takes emotional (and often physical) sweat and grit to find that Light and move ourselves toward it.

The Light in the darkness is the lesson, the growth moment, the unexpected window, the new way, the Sign. When life is dark, we can only see that Light if we believe it is there and are willing to search for it.

This is why real Gratitude also requires humility, the ability to look at ourselves and be willing to see that our vision may not have been in line with our Divine Path and that we always have more to learn. It forces us to acknowledge our blind spots, to become aware that we can't always see what's best in us and what's best for us.

Real Gratitude is being receptive and trusting.

Look Back Humbly

WHENEVER WE STAND POISED at the threshold of the old and the new, it's always worth remembering that we can't look forward without understanding what is behind us but can't move forward if we are trapped by what is behind us.

There's a fine line between reflection and rumination, between sifting through the past to absorb the nuggets of wisdom and experience and letting ourselves get caught up in perceived mistakes, missed opportunities, and perhaps bitterness or resentment.

That line lies in Humility.

Humility looks back and asks: what have I been taught about myself? About how to improve myself? About how I can grow?

Pride looks back and asks: who has wronged me? How can the world do this to me?

Fear looks back and asks: how can I ensure I am never exposed to risk, shame, or uncertainty again?

One of the distinguishing features of humility is Gratitude. The ability to practice the hard gratitude that comes with Faith: faith that what we experience is a tool to empower us in the future. And that future is just around the corner.

Reflecting with humility and gratitude promotes receptiveness and opens us up to what will come. It also empowers us to live purposefully, intentionally, and with direction.

When we reflect with humility and gratitude, we walk on the shoulders of giants - the shoulders of our past selves who elevate us, if we let them, to new heights.

Humility

HUMILITY GETS MIXED REVIEWS in our society. It's associated first and foremost with false humility, as well as with self-abasement or lack of self-confidence. And we tend to prefer that to the absence of humility.

In this superficial, everyday sense, humility is usually defined as 'not thinking too highly of yourself; not over-estimating your importance.' Unsurprisingly, this is a misleading interpretation of a beautiful, empowering element in our relationship with the Divine.

The Yoga Sutras tell us that Humility lies in relinquishing the illusion of control, Ishvara pranidhana (2.45), in cultivating trust in the process unfolding behind us, around us, and before. This is different from accepting that we are not important: it means accepting that our importance lies in that we are part of that process.

We are not separate. We are not above or below the process or others around us. We are not more or less divine than anyone or anything else. We are all divine beings with an innate capacity for greatness. We are all part of the process, each in a unique, divine way.

When we accept that we are one with the process, we can find stillness within it and gain insight into it.

In English, 'humility' comes from the Latin *humus*: earth. Embodying Humility means embodying the journey we make as we rise from the Earth, as the Earth sustains us; as we return to the Earth.

We are one with the source, with the journey, and with the destination.

Suffering

Yoga holds beautiful, life-affirming, and challenging lessons for us, both on and off the mat. Yoga Sutra 2.16 embodies this very deeply.

Heyam dukham anagram

Pain that has not yet come can be avoided.

On the surface, this Sutra suggests living a blessedly happy life, free from suffering, if we remain consistent with our physical and spiritual yogic practices. And this feels partly true: by maximizing the health of our physical body, inviting fresh energy into our lives with breathing practices, and reaching insight into ourselves and our connection with the Divine, we can reduce the impact of certain painful elements on our lives, like anxiety, or fear, or ill-health. We can avoid some suffering.

But not all suffering. Some suffering is overwhelming, unexpected, and unavoidable in the physical sense. We cannot turn away from it. We cannot prevent the tears from flowing. Suffering is, after all, one of the three essential characteristics of existence.

But Sutra 2.16 teaches us that real healing happens before the suffering begins. It is preemptive and empowering. Through a deep and consistent spiritual practice, we learn the mindfulness to be present in this moment and not bring pain onto ourselves by getting wrapped up in future suffering; the awareness that suffering is one of the great teachers, and a sacred part of our journeys which often brings with it the most important and transformational lessons; and the truth of impermanence, alongside the faith that suffering too, shall pass.

Suffering can, therefore, be avoided when we can receive it in its truth: just like *sukha* (joy, bliss), it is a sacred element of the human experience.

Stability

STABILITY IS OFTEN ASSOCIATED with immobility:

If I am stable, nothing can move me. Others cannot move me, tiredness, or changes in the world around me.

We apply this to our physical bodies, seeking stability in our asanas, and our mental and emotional well-being, building defenses around our minds and feelings.

This definition of stability felt wrong to me. It invites both physical and mental rigidity, locking out our joints and shoring up our emotional landscape — two things that can be very harmful.

Patanjali teaches us something different about stability. In Sutras 2.46-48, we learn that *"a yoga posture must possess the qualities of stability and ease. You practice asana by applying appropriate effort and contemplating the Infinite. And as a result, then you become undisturbed by life's challenges."*

Being undisturbed by life's challenges doesn't mean they don't affect us, whether sneezing in Bird of Paradise or facing an unexpected obstacle off the mat.

In kinesiology — the study of the body — stability means the ability to return to your orientation after a perturbation. And that is what I believe Patanjali is describing. Stability is not about resisting perturbation but being able to absorb it and return to ourselves. When we have Stability, life's challenges cannot diverge us from our path. Whatever comes our way, we can always reorientate ourselves.

True Stability is about being so Grounded that we cannot be uprooted, no matter how much we flow, how much we bend, how much we are pushed. Grounded in the Earth, which nurtures us, and in our connection with the Divine, elevating us towards our Purpose.

Journeying

LIFE ISN'T JUST ABOUT the journey — it IS a journey. It is not always a literal movement from one physical place to another but an emotional, mental, and spiritual flow onward. When we are living, we are never stationary. We are always in motion.

It's like a river. Sometimes, we flow openly and fast. Sometimes, we drift peacefully. Sometimes, we're bogged down or churning over rapids. But we're always moving. Even when we feel like we're moving backward, reverting to patterns we thought we'd outgrown, it's still not the same. Even those experiences are shaped by what we know now that we didn't know before.

And just like you can never step in the same river twice, no one ever meets the same you twice. That makes beautiful, trusting, and life-affirming relationships so amazing: no matter how long we've known certain people, be it family or friends, we've experienced each other's growth, celebrated successes, and supported each other through the challenges.

Though the river is familiar every time we meet, we're excited to see how it's grown, changed, and transformed.

Having those spaces where we know our growth is supported is so important—a spiritual and emotional home where we are encouraged to journey and celebrate when we grow.

Just as necessary, we need to give ourselves the space and compassion to grow. We must remain flexible in who we think we are and how we engage with the world. Being open to the fact that our journey might change us is the first step to experiencing that journey fully.

Mudras

SANSKRIT FOR 'SEAL,' 'GESTURE,' or 'mark,' Mudras are a subtle but powerful part of yogic practice that we can engage with in our daily lives.

Like asanas, mudras are poses, or gestures, that we usually express through our hands and help channel the subtle body's energy flows. They help to restore balance within the Koshas and guide our energy through our upper chakras, bringing light to our connection with the Divine.

We often use mudras, sometimes without even being consciously aware that we are doing so, during pranayama or meditations. They are frequently referred to as an external expression of inner resolve.

More than this, though, mudras are a central element in Ayurvedic healing. Within Ayurvedic thought, diseases are born from an imbalance in our body of one of the five key elements: space, air, fire, water, and earth. Each of these elements is represented by a finger:

- Air (Vayu)- Index Finger

- Fire (Agni)- Thumb Finger

- Water (Jal)- Little Finger

- Earth (Prithvi)- Ring Finger

- Space (Akash)- Middle Finger

Harnessing the power of mudras to channel the flows of energy that balance each element, therefore creating space for healing, both in our minds and bodies.

While mudras can be a core part of our practice, they can also help us channel our energy and balance our elements as we go about our daily lives. When we respond to imbalances, which inevitably arise during the hustle and bustle of the day, by focusing on a mudra, then on the physical sensation of our hands and our breath as energy is channeled and rebalanced, we empower ourselves to heal and grow both on and off the mat.

Shadow

WE ALL HAVE A shadow. A darker corner of ourselves that hides all those aspects of us we feel are inappropriate — those we feel ashamed or guilty about.

That shadow is often filled with our sadness, anger, or laziness, but it can also be where we hide our independence, personal power, emotions, and sensitivity. We are often made to feel that these parts of us are too much.

This shows that our shadow isn't our 'bad' side, as often suggested. It's simply the side that we are made to feel wrong about that is reflected to us as unfavorable in the eyes of this society.

But our shadow is part of our truth, and as such, it is part of our divine connection to the Universe. We simply need to shift our perspective: our shadow is there to teach us how to be whole and love ourselves.

Once, a student told me about her experience connecting to her shadow. Rather than viewing her shadow-self as unfavorable, she saw it as positive — the quiet guide "sewn to your feet," as she said. This perspective resonated powerfully with me.

Our shadow is our guide: learning to know, accept, and then celebrate. Our shadow teaches us emotional fluency so we can communicate better with ourselves and others. It teaches us that what others want us to see as negative, is actually a gift.

Anger is how we learn about setting boundaries. Sadness is how we learn about letting go. Laziness is how we learn what motivates us. Emotional sensitivity is how we learn about impact.

Embracing our shadow is how we receive those gifts.

Pranayama
Pause

Udgeeth Pranayama

"Deep, Rhythmic Chanting Breath"

This simple yet powerful breathing technique in yoga involves chanting the sound of "Om" while exhaling. It is a form of deep, resonant breathing that helps to calm the mind, reduce stress, and enhance overall well-being. Spiritually, Udgeeth Pranayama can bring about a trance-like awareness and create a sense of unity between us and the universe. Here's how to practice Udgeeth Pranayama:

1. Find a comfortable seated position: Sit on a yoga mat or cushion with your spine straight and your shoulders relaxed. You can sit cross-legged or on a chair, whichever is more comfortable for you.

2. Close your eyes and take a few deep breaths: Inhale deeply through your nose, filling your belly, chest, and lungs. Exhale fully, letting go of any tension or stress. Take a few moments to relax and center yourself.

3. Begin the practice: Take a deep breath in through your nose, filling your lungs completely.

4. Chant "Om" while exhaling: As you exhale, slowly and audibly chant the sound of "Om" (pronounced as "Aum"). Allow the sound to resonate from your throat and fill the space around you. The exhalation should be long, smooth, and controlled.

5. Focus on the vibration and sound: As you chant "Om" during the exhalation, pay attention to the vibration and sound it creates within your body. Feel the resonance in your throat, chest, and abdomen.

6. Repeat the practice: Continue this cycle of deep inhalation and chanting "Om" during the exhalation. Take your time with each breath, allowing the sound to flow naturally and effortlessly.

7. Maintain a relaxed and steady rhythm: Find a pace that feels comfortable for you. The inhalation should be deep and nourishing, while the exhalation with the "Om" chant should be gentle and soothing.

8. Practice for a specific duration: Start with practicing Udgeeth Pranayama for a shorter duration, such as 5-10 minutes, and gradually increase the time as you become more comfortable. You can set a timer or use a guided meditation app to help you keep track of the time.

9. End with relaxation: After completing the practice, sit quietly for a few moments, observing the effects of Udgeeth

Pranayama on your body and mind. Allow yourself to relax and integrate the benefits of the practice.

Part Thirteen

Integrate

IF THE GOAL OF yoga is the unity of the whole being, then Integration is the heart of our practice.

We talk about integration a lot in yoga, especially when it comes to solidifying new learning, new knowledge, and new practices — but integration isn't just what we should do with our new understanding.

It's central to acquiring that new knowledge in the first place, learning and growing in our practice, and making sure we're fully present on the mat.

Integration means involving every part of the body and mind in creating our asana, from our breath to our mantras and from our core to the tips of our fingers.

When we flow through our asanas, no part of our body or mind works in isolation. No part of ourselves gets left behind. Yoga is the journey that teaches us to see and work with every aspect of ourselves.

Most importantly, yoga is never about fighting any part of ourselves. Whether it's parts of our body that struggle with a particular asana, or parts of our mind that make it difficult to focus, yoga is never a battle against these elements. On the contrary, it's about seeing them, accepting them, and loving them so that they can be brought into our flow. In this way, we can work towards the unity of our whole being.

That's what I mean when I talk about Integration in yoga — bringing all of ourselves on this beautiful journey of growth and self-discovery.

Discipline and Structure

I THINK OF YOGA as a spiritual discipline that focuses on the Unity of the Being, bringing together body, breath, mind, and spirit to be in a beautiful connection with the Divine. It's not something you can just think about; it's something you must live and be with your whole Self.

Tapas is a powerful word I connect with the discipline of yoga. It's often translated to 'austerity,' specifically a type of discipline associated with the inner fire and heat that drives us. This is the force behind the spiritual discipline of yoga, which guides us to free the mind from fluctuations and superficial desires. It is a practice and a journey.

We often create a Structure for ourselves to deepen that practice and journey. Discipline and Structure seem to go hand in hand: without discipline, you cannot keep Structure; without Structure, you cannot deepen Discipline.

But one doesn't automatically feed into the other. We can practice yoga every day and still be completely spun out.

Simply making time for a yoga class, while an excellent place to start, is rarely enough. It's not just about showing up, but also *how* you show up.

It's your Intentionality that creates that connection between Discipline and Structure. Mindlessly following a structure we set for ourselves is not the same as Being within that Structure, so every breath we take and asana we flow through is guided by Tapas, by our inner fire.

Intentionality underlies everything we do. We must be present in the *why:* Why am I creating this structure? Why am I practicing tapas?

When we can answer these questions with our entire Self, our Discipline and Structure are united.

Excuses and Commitments

IT CAN FEEL GOOD to commit yourself. In the moment, we feel energized and optimistic. And then...a window often opens for the excuses to start flowing in.

Excuses are understandable and natural. They're the mind's loud fear response in the face of change, the Ego shouting its resistance to detachment. Or the Soul whispering that this commitment didn't come from a place of Truth. You can usually feel the difference because the Ego yells and screams while the Soul whispers and waits.

The first way to manage this flow of excuses is to make sure the commitments you're making to yourself come from a place of Soul, of Truth. This requires us to be honest with ourselves, honest about what we want and what our priorities are.

Did I commit to this because I thought I should? Because I was scared of not doing so? Or because I know it will help me thrive? Because it will help me arrive where I want to be?

When our commitments are aligned with our Souls, this is *Vrata* — vow, resolve, devotion; a deliberate, mindful commitment to follow through, to start, and repeat the actions that will increase our well-being.

But Vrata goes beyond devotion, beyond love. In her analysis of the Ramayana, Rebekah Boatrite wrote: *commitment is not always made from a place of love but instead from a place of duty.*

Commitment is dharma.

Our duty to grow. Our duty to take risks. Our duty to work for our betterment and of those around us. There are no excuses in the face of this commitment — only growth, learning, journeys, and results.

Growing in the Silence

WE'RE OFTEN MADE TO feel like Silence is a failure like we should fill every waking moment with Sound, Action, Results, or some other illusion of productivity. In this day and age of constant over-stimulation, Silence can also feel strange and anxiety-inducing.

But one of the most important lessons of yoga is *Mouna*, the Sanskrit word for Silence. Mouna brings insight into that which is beyond words and, as such, is a vital practice for gaining an understanding of ourselves and the Divine.

Swami Sivananda said: *"By practicing mouna, the energy of speech is slowly transmuted into spiritual energy."* For me, this is connected to the fifth limb of Patanjali's Raja Yoga, *pratyahara*, the practice of drawing the senses inward. As the world around us continues to get busier and busier and faster and faster, pratyahara is our path to inner peace.

This has been especially relevant to my growth as a teacher. When I began teaching, I felt I had to keep talking or cueing to fill the empty space between my words. I was afraid that the silence in between cues or while in a posture would deter students from presence. But it was when I stopped talking and invited silence that real presence happened.

Mouna is that Space where we absorb, where we integrate, where we connect. Everything we learn as we do is connected to the Soul when we practice Mouna. This is the only way we can honor the fifth limb of yoga, making Silence central to a holistic yoga practice and a holistic, intentional, and aware Life.

Do What You're Created to Do

OUR LIGHT SHINES BRIGHTEST when we are true to ourselves. But being true to ourselves is one of the hardest things we can do. There's so much noise around us: people's expectations, people's approval, the role models we have — or don't have — available.

All that noise can get in the way of understanding ourselves. If we don't understand our truth, how can we let it shine?

> *"The Sun doesn't ask for God's approval to shine. It only does what it's created to do."*

We often feel that our true nature needs to be approved by others or that we need to form ourselves into what others expect us to be. But our true nature is just that: our truth. It's inevitable, unstoppable, and undeniable. It's what we were born to be.

Our Light moves us. It moves through us and Shines out of us. Trying to dim its radiance harms us and deprives the world of something beautiful.

When intimately acquainted with it, we can most powerfully and impactfully let our truth shine. When we see it, feel it, and know it inside and out.

Retreating from the noise, withdrawing from the voices that tell us who or what we should be, helps us find our truth. When we can create an island of Silence amidst a sea of noise, we can shine like the Sun.

Remember

LIVING IN THE PAST can lead to inertia and a loss of connection. Living in the future can have much the same impact.

When we're so focused on analyzing what was or what might be, when we get so comfortable in who we were that we lose track of who we're becoming, when we get afraid of who we might become that we turn our back on who we are---then we go nowhere. We lose that connection to the moment, which makes our life and relationships intimate and awake.

The trick is to keep our gaze on both: to have one eye on the past and one on the future while our heart lives the present to the fullest degree.

Bettering ourselves requires us to take a bird's eye view of our path, understanding what worked and didn't, what we can take with us, and what we should release. To visualize how our current path might lead to where we need to be.

But bettering ourselves also means being in the present. Experiencing the sacred nature of this life as it is now.

In Patanjali's Yoga Sutras, the ultimate goal of yoga is to move beyond the ego, to pull back the veil, and find ourselves inhabiting the nature of the Purusha, cosmic consciousness. The practice of yoga is, therefore, about more than simply living fully in the present. It's about understanding that the present is also where the Divine lives.

You encounter the Divine in every moment. You abide in the nature of the Purusha with every breath.

Playful

LIFE CAN BE CHALLENGING, and confronting, and overwhelming, and stressful. But do not become rigid. Do not shut yourself off from living this life.

Because you are playful.

As adults, we often forget about the importance of play. We get swept up in wave after wave of productivity, achievement, deadlines, duties, practicalities, and looking after others. Self-care is frequently a neglected practice, and Play is a very overlooked aspect of self-care.

But adding playfulness into our lives brings joy, presence, freedom, and release. It gives us the space to pause and shed some of the seriousness so we can walk lighter into our challenges.

Most importantly, when we forget how to be playful, we also forget how to grow. Where fear of failure says: I can't do this, Play says: I can try, and I can laugh, and I can try again.

Approaching life with a playful attitude helps us to build resilience so that we can express and manifest ourselves fearlessly.

Adding play into our lives also helps us to help others. If we're walking lighter, laughing more, healing faster, and being more present, we are also helping others do so. When we draw others into our Play, we raise our vibrations. When we Play, we have the power to create Light.

Doubt

THE BUDDHA DEFINES DOUBT, *samshaya,* as indecision or skepticism. While a questioning mind is a powerful tool in healthy doses, Doubt can attract fear and uncertainty when we find ourselves out of balance. It has a sneaky way of making us immobile, keeping us stuck where we are when our Soul is yearning for us to live in Alignment with our intuition, with the Divine.

In this sense, Doubt is a tool of the Ego. When the Ego is undermined as we step into our Power and true lives, it responds by trying to regain control. It paralyzes us with Doubt, ensuring we stay and stagnate in our comfort zone, where the Ego is the boss.

It's as if, through Doubt, the Ego cuts off or limits our Prana, our vital life energy. We become indecisive and passive, characterized by the inability to take action — and though we are immobile, we are not in Stillness.

Doubt is one of the biggest obstacles we must overcome on our journey towards living in alignment with our truth. To my mind, the cure prescribed by the Buddha is the most beautiful and straightforward principle: *shraddha*, faith.

Not blind faith. We are not being called to follow the teachings of others mindlessly. Faith in ourselves. Faith in our Intuition. Faith in our Truth. Faith in our connection to the Divine. When we have faith that the thread connecting us to the Sacred shines bright, we can let our Soul take flight.

Darsana

SOMETIMES, THINGS HAPPEN IN life that leave us feeling unsettled, like we're walking on uneven ground that moves beneath our feet, and we might feel unsure of our feelings, roles, or goals.

In these times, returning to the yoga Darsanas is helpful. In Hindu philosophy, there are six darsanas, 'visions' or 'ways of seeing the world' in Sanskrit, and yoga darsanas are some of the most ancient. A yoga darsana is how we can answer the question: "What *do I choose to do with the gift of my most precious life?*"

When we spend time meditating on this question, breathing into it, flowing through our asanas, and sitting in silence with it, we give ourselves the time and space to reconnect with who we are when our mind, heart, and soul unite and what might be possible for us when we can flow in this state both on and off the mat.

When we do this, we also give ourselves the space to find that alignment that we may have lost, to notice where we diverged from our values and priorities, and to reconnect with them.

A rich abundance of yoga darsanas can help us find ourselves. Some invite us to see past everyday life's false perceptions, freeing ourselves from mistaken identification. Others remind us to explore embodiment as the gift of the Divine, grounding us in the moment. There are yoga darsanas that lean into emptiness and others into fullness; darsanas for suffering, and darsanas for bliss. There is a darsana for you.

Self-Reflection

Svadhyaya, derived from the Sanskrit words "sva" meaning self and "adhyaya" meaning study, is the practice of self-study and self-reflection. It encourages us to explore our inner world, understand our thoughts, emotions, and actions, and ultimately grow into our best selves.

In our fast-paced lives, it's easy to get caught up in the external chaos and forget to nurture our inner being. Svadhyaya reminds us to step back, pause, and observe ourselves with love and curiosity.

By dedicating time to self-reflection, we better understand our strengths, weaknesses, and patterns. We become aware of our limiting beliefs and can consciously work towards transforming them into empowering ones. Svadhyaya helps us break free from self-imposed limitations and embrace our true potential.

But how can we incorporate Svadhyaya into our daily lives? Here are a few simple practices that have worked wonders for me:

- Journaling: Set aside a few minutes daily to write down your thoughts, feelings, and experiences. This self-expression allows you to gain clarity, release emotions, and uncover hidden insights.

- Meditation: Find a quiet space, close your eyes, and connect with your breath. As you observe your thoughts without judgment, you'll develop a deeper understanding of your mind's patterns and tendencies.

- Reading and Learning: Engage in books, podcasts, or courses that inspire personal growth. Explore different perspectives, philosophies, and teachings to expand your knowledge and challenge your beliefs.

- Seeking Feedback: Reach out to trusted friends, mentors, or coaches for constructive feedback. Their insights can provide valuable perspectives and help you identify blind spots.

Remember, Svadhyaya is not about self-criticism or judgment. It's about cultivating self-awareness, self-acceptance, and self-love. It's a journey of self-discovery that allows us to align with our authentic selves and live a more fulfilling life.

Pranayama
Pause

Nadi Shodhana Pranayama

"Alternate Nostril Breathing"

Nadi Shodhana, also known as alternate nostril breathing, is a pranayama technique in yoga that helps balance the energy channels in the body. Nadi Shodhana can be practiced at any time, but it is particularly beneficial in the morning to start your day with a clear and balanced mind. It can also be practiced before meditation or to calm the mind during stressful situations.

A regular practice of Nadi Shodhana improves focus, concentration, and memory. It also cleanses the energy channels by helping to remove any blockages or impurities in the energy channels, allowing the life force energy (prana) to flow freely.

Here is a step-by-step guide on how to practice Nadi Shodhana:

1. Find a comfortable seated position: Sit cross-legged on the floor or a cushion. Make sure your spine is straight and your shoulders are relaxed.

2. Relax your left hand: Rest your left hand on your left knee, with the palm facing upward. You can use jnana mudra by touching the tip of your index finger to the tip of your thumb.

3. Use your right hand: Bring your right hand up towards your face. Place your index and middle fingers between your eyebrows, lightly pressing on your third eye point. Rest your ring finger on your left nostril and your thumb on your right nostril.

4. Close your eyes: Close your eyes gently and take a few deep breaths to relax your body and mind.

5. Start with the left nostril: Close your right nostril with your thumb and inhale deeply through your left nostril. Count to four as you inhale.

6. Switch nostrils: Close your left nostril with your ring finger, release your thumb from the right nostril, and exhale slowly through the right nostril. Count to eight as you exhale.

7. Inhale through the right nostril: Inhale deeply through the right nostril, counting to four.

8. Switch nostrils again: Close your right nostril with your thumb, release your ring finger from the left nostril, and

exhale slowly through the left nostril. Count to eight as you exhale.

9. Repeat the cycle: This completes one round of Nadi Shodhana. Continue alternating between the nostrils, inhaling for four counts and exhaling for eight counts. Aim to complete 5-10 rounds, or practice for 5-10 minutes.

Part Fourteen

Frustration

CERTAIN EMOTIONS CAN BE perceived as 'negative,' leading us to try and hide or suppress them. This can be especially true in some spiritual communities, where the 'toxic positivity' phenomenon might make us feel guilty for experiencing or engaging with these feelings.

But Ghandi said,

> *"It is not that I do not get angry. I don't give vent to my anger."*

We need to understand that feeling sad, angry, or frustrated is not' un-yogic.' They're just as much a part of our spiritual journey as happiness, love, and joy. The lesson truly lies in how we teach ourselves to manage, express, and release these emotions.

While uncomfortable and unpleasant, frustration is a sign that something is off. The way we are doing things needs to be fixed. We need to try something new.

Frustration is an invitation to wake up.

At the core of our biochemistry, when our brain registers frustration, it releases neurochemicals alerting our nervous system that a change is needed.

And when we make small adjustments, tweak our balance, shift our perspective, and reach for support, our brain sends out little dopamine hits, helping us continue to make changes even while we're struggling.

Frustration is not an end to learning or achieving. It is the beginning.

Frustration is an invitation to embrace the laughter and joy of the journey, making it a vital part of the learning process. We feel the feeling, make a change, get a hit of dopamine until our goal is achieved or our misconceptions are revealed, and then we feel liberation, joy, and accomplishment.

Avidya: Perception

AVIDYA REFERS TO WRONG seeing or incorrect perception and teaches us that our suffering often arises from our attachment to how things should be. We create space for fresh perspectives when we release these expectations and let go of our preconceived notions.

In yoga, we approach each pose with curiosity and openness, allowing our bodies to guide us rather than forcing ourselves into a predetermined shape. By letting go of how things should look, we can truly see and appreciate the beauty and uniqueness of each moment.

Avidya invites us to tap into our intuition and trust our inner guidance. Instead of relying solely on external appearances, we can cultivate a deeper connection with ourselves and the world by tuning into how things feel. In yoga, we learn to listen to our bodies, honor our limits, and balance effort and ease. By intuitively feeling our way through life, we can make choices that align with our authentic selves, leading to greater fulfillment and contentment.

By practicing Avidya, we can cultivate clarity and authenticity in our lives. When we let go of our fixed perceptions and embrace the present moment, we open ourselves to new possibilities and experiences. We learn to see beyond the surface and connect with the essence of things. Through yoga, we develop a heightened awareness of our bodies, minds, and emotions, allowing us to navigate life with greater clarity and authenticity.

Just as yoga teaches us to approach each pose with an open mind and heart, let us approach life with the same curiosity and openness. Notice the power of perception and watch as your world transforms into a tapestry of clarity, authenticity, and profound connection.

Pivots

YOU'RE NEVER STUCK. YOU'RE never too old. You've never come too far.

Pivoting on our trajectory can sometimes feel and look like a failure. Or it might be absolutely terrifying. We were heading one way, and suddenly, for one reason or another, we were not.

In life, as in yoga, there are moments to be powerfully grounded down, and there are moments to be light on our toes and in our minds. Being light, flexible, and unattached to specific outcomes means we have the adaptability and strength to take on whatever life throws at us.

It means we can recognize when it's time to learn something new. Something different.

No matter where you are in life or how old you are, no matter how much you have planned out, there will come a time when the Universe asks you to make a change.

This is not a failure. It is an invitation to grow. And while it might be terrifying, it is an invitation to show ourselves we are worthy of courage.

It takes strength. The kind of strength we find within ourselves when we close our eyes and immerse ourselves in our breathing, in our core. The strength that says:

Yes. I can learn. Yes. I can grow. Thank you for calling me to spread my wings.

If you are facing the deep knowledge that something needs to change, I invite you to take a moment and listen. Why are you feeling this way? What is this new path you are learning? What does it feel like? Where can it lead that your current path does not? Let go of the resistance and let yourself discover this newness and change you are being called to.

Disciplined Mind

IN OUR JOURNEY TOWARDS spiritual growth and self-realization, a disciplined mind acts as our guiding light. It helps us navigate through the chaos of life and find inner peace. By applying the lessons of The Bhagavad Gita, a revered Hindu scripture, we can embark on a transformative journey toward inner harmony and enlightenment.

Moments of undisciplined minds can manifest in various ways. For example, our minds often wander, getting caught up in trivial matters or external stimuli. The Gita teaches us to focus on the present moment, letting go of distractions, and staying centered on our spiritual path.

Or maybe we find ourselves attached to outcomes, often becoming fixated on the results of our actions, leading to anxiety and disappointment. The Gita reminds us to detach ourselves from outcomes, perform our duties selflessly, and surrender to the divine will.

Often, too, our minds can be consumed by negative thoughts, self-doubt, and judgment. The Gita encourages us to cultivate positive thinking, self-compassion, and mindfulness, allowing us to transcend negativity and embrace inner peace.

By applying these lessons, we can nurture a disciplined mind and embark on a transformative journey towards self-realization. Daily practices like meditation, yoga, and self-reflection are essential to discipline our minds and experience the profound wisdom within us.

Remember, the Bhagavad Gita teaches us that spiritual growth is a personal journey, and each step we take toward discipline and self-realization brings us closer to our true selves. Let's embrace the power of a disciplined mind and unlock the infinite potential within us.

Action Without Attachments to Results

"You have the right to your actions but never to your actions' fruits. Act for the action's sake. And do not be attached to inaction. Self-possessed, resolute, act without any thought of results, open to success or failure. This equanimity is Yoga."

IN THE BHAGAVAD GITA, Krishna imparts profound wisdom to Arjuna, teaching him the art of action without attachments to results. This timeless teaching holds immense relevance in our modern lives, reminding us to embrace the journey and release our fixation on outcomes.

The Bhagavad Gita teaches us that true fulfillment lies in the process, not just the end result. When we detach from the outcome, we can fully immerse ourselves in the present moment and give our best to every action we take. By focusing on the journey, we cultivate a sense of purpose, passion, and dedication, allowing us to experience a deeper connection with our actions and the world around us.

We free ourselves from expectations when we release our attachment to specific outcomes. This liberation brings peace and contentment, as we no longer measure our worth solely by external achievements. Instead, we find fulfillment in the process, embracing the lessons, growth, and experiences that come our way. By surrendering to the flow of life, we open ourselves up to infinite possibilities and allow the universe to guide us toward our highest potential.

The Bhagavad Gita reminds us to trust in the universe's divine order. Just as Krishna guided Arjuna, we, too, can find solace in surrendering to a higher power. By relinquishing our need for control and surrendering to the universe's wisdom, we align ourselves with the natural flow of life. This surrender allows us to navigate challenges gracefully, knowing that everything happens for a reason.

By focusing on the journey, letting go of expectations, and surrendering to the divine order, we can experience a profound shift in our perspective. We find freedom, peace, and fulfillment in every action we take, knowing that outcomes do not solely determine our worth.

Equanimity

ACTING OUT OF ANGER only harms yourself. Yelling at someone to convince them that you're right means that even if you win the argument, you still lose because of the residual damage done to yourself and your relationship.

Instead, learn how to disengage whenever you're off your spiritual center with the humble recognition that you cannot see clearly when you are emotionally flooded. Emotions are like storms in the emotional sky that obscure your clarity. How can you engage in enlightened action if you can't see straight? I know how hard it is to disengage amid a heated exchange or not take the emotional bait in an argument. I've gotten into more than my fair share of disagreements that ended bitterly.

Equanimity.

In many ways, this is the antidote to anger. Called *Upekshanam* in Sanskrit, the Yoga Sutras advise yogis to cultivate an equanimous mind in the presence of anyone or anything we designate as evil or wrong, essentially anything that gets our blood boiling. It's a humble teaching but one that can transform your life.

Once your mind is calm, you see clearly and can wait for the appropriate action and response to be revealed. If you could see, for example, that the person who cut you off in traffic is being rude because their dog just died, would you forgive them or honk at them? If you could see that your partner is hurting because of a stressful day when they snap at you, would you snap back at them or hug them? Jarvis Masters wrote in *Finding Freedom* that as long as we are all a bunch of angry faces shouting at each other, the world will never be peaceful.

So, for today, ask yourself where you have been acting out of your anger, righteous indignation, or just a feeling that the other person was wrong. See if you can take a step back and cultivate equanimity instead. It takes great strength to drop the fight and walk away. Then, once you regain your calm mind, ask for guidance about the next step and wait to act until you come from a place of love.

Sthira and Sukha

IN ANCIENT YOGIC PHILOSOPHY, the concepts of Sthira and Sukha hold immense wisdom. Sthira represents stability, strength, and resilience, while Sukha embodies ease, comfort, and joy. These qualities are not limited to the yoga mat but can be applied to our everyday lives, helping us find balance and contentment.

Just like a tree with deep roots, we, too, can cultivate resilience by nurturing our physical, mental, and emotional well-being. Regular exercise, a balanced diet, and quality sleep contribute to physical stability. Engaging in activities that challenge our minds, such as reading or learning new skills, helps us build mental strength. Embracing emotional intelligence and practicing mindfulness can enhance our emotional stability, allowing us to gracefully navigate life's ups and downs.

Sukha reminds us to seek ease and joy in our daily experiences. It encourages us to let go of unnecessary stress and embrace moments of contentment. Taking time for self-care, whether indulging in a warm bath, reading a book, or spending time in nature, allows us to recharge and find inner peace. Cultivating gratitude by acknowledging and appreciating the simple pleasures in life can bring immense joy. By consciously focusing on the positive aspects of our lives, we invite more happiness and fulfillment into our everyday existence.

The key lies in finding a harmonious balance between Sthira and Sukha. Too much stability without flexibility can lead to rigidity and stagnation, while excessive ease without discipline can result in complacency. We create a foundation that supports growth, resilience, and contentment by integrating both qualities. It's about recognizing when to push ourselves out of our comfort zones, embracing challenges, and adapting to change while also allowing ourselves moments of rest, relaxation, and celebration.

Strive to embody the qualities of Sthira and Sukha, both on and off the yoga mat, and create a grounded, joyful, and fulfilling life. By cultivating stability and strength, we become better equipped to face life's challenges. Simultaneously, by seeking ease and joy, we enhance our overall well-being and find fulfillment in the present moment. Embrace this delicate balance and watch your life transform into a beautiful dance of strength and serenity.

Individuality

IN A WORLD THAT often tries to fit us into molds and labels, it's essential to remember that our true strength lies in embracing our authentic selves. We are all beautifully unique, with our quirks, passions, and dreams that make us who we are.

Break free from the chains of conformity and let your individuality shine brightly. Embrace your passions, whether they're considered "mainstream" or not. Pursue your dreams, even if they seem unconventional.

Remember, our differences make the world a vibrant and diverse place. Each one of us has something special to offer, a unique perspective that can inspire and uplift others.

Don't be afraid to stand out from the crowd, to be unapologetically yourself. Embrace your quirks, your flaws, and your strengths, for they are what make you truly extraordinary.

Celebrate your individuality and support one another in our journeys of self-discovery. Together, we can create a world where everyone feels empowered to be their authentic selves.

So, shine your brightest, radiating love, kindness, and acceptance for ourselves and others. Inspire others to embrace their individuality and celebrate the beautiful tapestry of humanity.

Remember, you are enough, just as you are. Embrace your uniqueness, and let it be your guiding light on this incredible journey called life.

Surrender

THE IDEA OF SURRENDER is easily misunderstood. The word calls up notions of 'giving up' and weakness or losing control and letting external influences dictate our lives. It's a notion that can make us fear powerlessness and vulnerability.

But without Surrender, we can never truly experience the moment. Nor can we ever truly participate in what the Universe offers us.

I like to think about Surrender less as 'giving up' and more as 'giving in'— giving in to the magic that is all around us, giving in to the moment so that we can experience it fully and without judgment, giving in to our truth.

And that takes strength and courage.

Our desire to control aspects of our lives means we spend most of our time analyzing the past while living in the future. This is where our Ego has convinced us we are safe and where our Ego wants us to stay. But it's only the illusion of understanding and control.

It means we cannot be receptive to the whispers of the Universe, to the yearnings of our Soul. Being in tune with our truth and the Sacred, means being open to what every moment and every breath has to tell us.

Surrender requires that we accept the past, taking from it the lessons that align best with our journeys and holding the future loosely, with no attachments or expectations. It is a dance where we learn to know our partner, the Sacred, the Universe, so well that without words and resistance, we make and re-make something beautiful together with every step we take.

Healing

HEALING IS IN THE small things, the precious moments, the beating of a heart, and the touch of a loved one.

Whether the chaos and turmoil are around us or within us, on a global scale or a personal level, it's by finding the stillness in those healing moments that we begin the process of re-centering.

Often, the first thing pain, chaos, and suffering take from us is the ability to see those moments in the first place. But they're everywhere and in abundance.

When you step onto your mat, it's not just about striking a pose or achieving physical flexibility; it's a profound journey of self-discovery and inner transformation—a time to consciously try to still your mind and see the Sacred. It is within this sacred space that we can find healing and restoration. You can take this into your everyday life—every step, every breath, it's much like a step onto your mat.

And when we take that chance, the chance of letting the chaos and the anxiety exist around us without judging it or ourselves, we see that they are hiding what is always within our reach: the Sacred.

We find acceptance once we can get in touch with the Sacred in the fabric of daily life.

Acceptance is an essential part of healing—what we cannot control, we can only accept. Once we accept it, we can approach any situation most constructively, in the way that will serve us best on our path.

Once we find acceptance, then we can find our center. In our center, we find healing.

Once we find our healing, we can heal the world.